AS Level General Studies

Society, Politics and the Economy

AQA

AS Level General Studies

Society, Politics and the Economy

John Barnes
Shaun Best
Rob Dransfield

Published in 2003 by:
Nelson Thornes Ltd
Delta Place
27 Bath Road
CHELTENHAM
GL53 7TH
United Kingdom

03 04 05 06 07 / 10 9 8 7 6 5 4 3 2 1

A catalogue record for this book is available from the British Library

ISBN 0 7487 7122 0

Page make-up by Northern Phototypesetting Co Ltd, Bolton

Printed and bound in Italy by Canale

contents

acknowledgements

The authors and publishers are grateful to the following for permission to reproduce material:

- American Federation of Labor-Congress of Industrial Organizations for the statistics on p.4.
- HarperCollins Publishers Ltd for the extract on p.51, from Horsman and Marshall (1994) *After the Nation-State: Citizens, Tribalism and the New World*, HarperCollins, pp.39–40.
- Keith Brannen for the extract on pp.107–108, from 'Extracts from the trial of William Peter Sutcliffe', www.execulink.com/~kbrannen/trialall.pdf.
- Routledge, Inc., part of the Taylor & Francis Group, for the quotes on pp.40–42, from Apple, M. (1979) *Ideology and Curriculum*, Routledge, pp.20, 40, 166–168, 173.
- Townsend, P. for 'The Deprivation Index' on p.18, from *Poverty in the United Kingdom*, Penguin, p.250.

Every effort has been made to contact copyright holders and we apologize if any have been overlooked. Should copyright have been unwittingly infringed in this book, the owners should contact the publishers, who will make corrections at reprint.

Photo credits:

- Art Directors and Trip Photolibrary (p.45, middle)
- Associated Press (p.1, bottom; p.89, bottom)
- BBC Picture Library (p.34, top; p.64, top and middle)
- Bubbles Photolibrary/Angela Hampton (p.64, middle)
- Bubbles Photolibrary/Jacqui Farrow (p.1, top middle and bottom middle)
- Bubbles Photolibrary/Jennie Woodcock (p.12, top middle)
- Bubbles Photolibrary/Louisjoy Thurston (p.1, top)
- Corbis/Bettman (p.73, top, top middle, bottom)
- Corbis/Ralph A Clevenger (p.112)
- Corel 461 (NT) (p.45, top)

- Mike Gunnill Photography (p.23, bottom)
- Offside Sports Photography (p.12, top)
- Photofusion/Joanne O'Brien (p.34, bottom)
- Photofusion/Maggie Murray(p.12, bottom)
- Photofusion/Paul Doyle (p.102, middle)
- Photofusion/Paula Solloway (p.23, bottom middle)
- Photofusion/Sam Tanner (p.12, bottom middle)
- Punch Cartoon Library (p.2)
- Rex Features Ltd (p.23, top and middle; p.34, middle; p.73, bottom middle; p74; p. 89, top and middle; p.94; p.102, top and bottom)
- Robert Harding Picture Library (p.45, bottom)

introduction

Meeting the assessment objectives and the nature of knowledge

Many students will be disappointed with their AS general studies results and may be confused as to the reason why they significantly underperformed. One possible reason for this underperformance is the very difficult and demanding nature of the AS general studies assessment objectives. In addition to providing the *right* answer, in any advanced-level examination the student must meet the assessment objectives in order to gain marks. Examiners find it difficult to write examination questions that meet all of the assessment objectives, teachers find it difficult to plan lessons to meet all of the assessment objectives and students may not be fully aware of the significance of the assessment objectives. So what are the assessment objectives and how do you meet them?

The overall assessment objectives for general studies

The overall objectives are:

- *AO1 (assessment objective 1)*: Demonstrate relevant knowledge and understanding applied to a range of issues, using skills from different disciplines.
- *AO2*: Communicate clearly and accurately in a concise, logical and relevant way.
- *AO3*: Marshal evidence and draw conclusions; select, interpret, evaluate and integrate information, data, concepts and opinions.
- *AO4*: Demonstrate understanding of different types of knowledge and of the relationship between them, appreciating their limitations.

The mark schemes allocate a number of marks for some or all of these objectives for each question, according to the nature of the question and what it is intended to test. A maximum of 15 marks can be awarded per question, consisting of up to four marks for each of AO1 to AO3 and up to six marks for AO4.

Some of the assessment objectives are reasonably clear: AO2 for example expects the student to write in an appropriate legible style, organize the information clearly and coherently, with accurate spelling, punctuation and grammar and with appropriate use of any necessary specialist vocabulary. However, AO4 is not so clear. Questions that test AO4 assess the students' understanding of the nature of knowledge itself. Knowledge about knowledge is not simply about the students outlining their knowledge of various subjects. Knowledge about knowledge involves making a distinction between 'first-order' knowledge (first-hand factual knowledge) and 'second-order' knowledge (knowledge about how we *know what we know*), the capacity to discern the differing nature of different types of knowledge, such as the difference between: scientific, aesthetic, propagandist and moral knowledge. To achieve AO4 successfully the student must make the very demanding philosophical shift from *knowing that* to *knowing how*.

In a nutshell, to gain all the available marks for AO4 you need to identify different *types* of knowledge. A common division is between:

- *objective knowledge* – knowledge that is based upon facts; and
- *subjective knowledge* – knowledge that is based upon something other than facts, such as a moral value, a religious belief, a political opinion or an opinion that is simply unsupported by facts or evidence.

The chapters in this book all contain a varied number of activities. The purpose of these sections is to give you opportunities to identify and evaluate the different types of knowledge that you will come across in the general studies examinations.

Personal knowledge – from *knowing that* to *knowing how*

A human being cannot make sense of information without it becoming personal – without having feelings about the information. We have to have the knowledge of how the things we are interested in work in order to function as people. We may have the knowledge that 'things' work in a particular way, but we may not have a complete knowledge of the underlying theoretical principles of *how* 'things' work in the way that they do. This personal knowledge has no obvious form of measurement, because it is based upon feelings and an understanding of oneself as a person: likes, dislikes, prejudices and the underlying motivation for these choices. This knowledge may be ambiguous and/or partial, based upon intuition and formed without real reasoning, but all of us have a perception of why things happen to us in the way that they do. Although this perception may not be based upon systematically gathered research findings, it is based upon the personal observation of causes and consequences that are real to us. We all have a need to know that provides us with a personal motivation to discover a reality beyond our safe subjectivity. This process of moving from our personal knowledge *that* to a more objective knowledge of *how* may bring us into conflict with widely shared conceptual frameworks – such as sociological perspectives or politica ideologies. When we construct knowledge of a situation or event and can justify the validity of our perceptions we can escape the pressure to conform and, as learners, escape the mere memorization of concepts that hold no personal value for us as learners. We have to relate personal knowledge from our own interactions to theories.

This is my view of what assessment objective AO4 is about, but how do we demonstrate, in an examination, that we have achieved it.

How do I meet A04?

In order to meet this objective, students attempting a question must look at the extracts provided by the examiner and answer the following questions about the content, irrespective of the wording of the question asked:

- Is the extract based upon personal experience or first-hand experience?
- Attempt to identify what is the underlying perspective of the author. Is the author a feminist, a Conservative, a Marxist or something else?
- Once you have identified the perspective of the authors, are there any general criticisms of their perspective that you could use to evaluate the arguments within the extract?
- Are there any alternative perspectives that you identify that are equally as valid?
- Are there any alternative perspectives that you find more convincing? If so, state what they are and why you find them more convincing.
- Are good examples used to highlight or support points made in the extract?
- Is the extract biased?
- Is the extract limited to one geographical area?
- Does the extract have a date? Is the date significant? Is the source recent? Has the situation changed since the extract was written?
- Does the extract make generalizations? Can any generalizations be justified?
- Does the extract make generalizations from a small sample of people?
- Is the extract based upon fact or opinion?
- Are the opinions in the extract supported by evidence or not?
- Is the source valid, in other words, does the extract give a complete picture? Or are there omissions of significant facts?
- Does the extract provide a balanced argument? Are there counter arguments that you can identify?

- Are the quotations within the extract reputable? Is the source quoted, for example a racist, a feminist or a socialist? Is the source from a newspaper with a political bias? Does the extract, or quotes within the extract, have any preconceptions that you can identify?
- Can you cite any evidence to support claims made within the extract?

So where did these assessment objectives come from?

In the 1980s there was a wide range of syllabuses, modes of assessment and exam boards. Staff could choose the syllabus and mode of assessment that they believed was in the interests of the students that they taught. Initially, the Schools Curriculum and Assessment Authority (SCAR) was formed to look at and approve qualifications. In 1996 Sir Ron Dearing published his review of qualifications for 16–19-year-olds. This led directly to the introduction of Curriculum 2000. In 1997, the Qualifications and Curriculum Authority (QCA) further reduced the number of qualifications and would only approve qualifications that met the QCA criteria. The QCA have overseen the introduction of key skills, the unitization of the courses into six modules, and the modularization of 'A' levels. Hence students doing 'A' levels will now take an examination at the end of the first year before progression into the second year. The QCA made examination boards merge and they became known as awarding bodies. This has further reduced the choice of syllabus and 'syllabuses' became 'specifications'. These new specifications contained new assessment objectives, and students had to demonstrate that they had competently achieved them in order to be awarded a pass at advanced level. By 2000, teaching staff in school sixth forms and further education colleges had to choose from an approved list of subject specifications, which were modular, which incorporated key skills that staff had to deliver within the subject, and which had QCA-devised and imposed assessment objectives. The QCA qualification framework places all 'general qualifications' – GCSEs and A and AS levels, vocationally related qualifications (including vocational A levels) and occupational qualifications (NVQs) into a formal system that ranks qualifications into a hierarchy and identifies progression routes, which is known as the national qualifications framework. All qualifications from GCSE to AVCE, AS and A2 level, now have rigid rules for assessment. In other words, if you or your teacher do not like the AOs of a particular specification you cannot shop around for something more appropriate.

Conclusion

The QCA's mission is to promote quality and coherence in education and training, in the interests of individuals, the economy and society. Although the assessment criteria are very demanding of the student, the criteria are transparent. In other words, students know how they are being assessed and by what criteria they are being assessed. This book will help you demonstrate your ability in the areas that the assessment criteria address.

1

Sex and gender

Before the twentieth century it was commonly assumed that social inequalities between men and women were biologically determined. Women were assumed to be naturally inferior to men. Differences in 'sex' were assumed to be the cause of a range of social inequalities. Men were assumed to be stronger, more aggressive, yet more rational and superior in intelligence, whereas women were assumed to be more caring in nature, primarily because of their 'natural' childbearing and childrearing roles. They were also thought to be more irrational and emotional. As a consequence women had far fewer legal rights, political rights and career opportunities than men.

Feminists were always highly sceptical of this argument. In 1971 Ann Oakley highlighted the significance of gender – our shared ideas of masculinity and femininity – and pointed to the ways in which gender roles (the roles that men and women play) varied, both over time and from place to place. In other words, according to the feminists, there is nothing inevitable about male or female behaviour. Gender roles were culturally defined and socially produced rather than biological in origin.

The socialization process starts at birth and ends with death. Individuals start to internalize their appropriate social roles, from the moment the midwife tells the parents if the child is a girl or a boy. From that moment parents, brothers and sisters, friends, school, the media and many other institutions impose upon us traditional ideologies about men being 'masculine' and women being 'feminine'.

Women's rights

In the nineteenth century, British women had very few rights, and feminism – the movement for social, economic and political equality between

key terms

socialization

Men and women were brought up to accept traditional gender roles through a pro-cess called 'socialization', an ongo-ing pro-cess of devel-opment in which people learn the values, atti-tudes and beliefs that make up the culture of their society.

men and women – has a long history. Towards the end of seventeenth century, perhaps because of the chaos brought about by the English civil war, there was a distinct increase in the production of social and political texts by women, particularly women from a working-class background. Many women were expressing their opinions about social and political issues in public for the first time. One such text was Mary Astell's (1694) 'A Serious Proposal to the Ladies', which criticized the institution of marriage and is unexpectedly 'modern' in both its tone and argument.

Women could not vote and, as Sir William Blackstone explained, 'By marriage, the husband and wife are one person in law: that is, the very being or legal existence of the woman is suspended during that marriage.' In practical terms this meant that, on marrying, normally 'both possession and control of a woman's property, including any monies she might earn from paid labour, passed to her husband' (Levine, 1987, p.134). It was only with the Matrimonial Causes Act 1857 that women obtained limited access to divorce, usually on a specific cause other than adultery. Women were also granted limited rights of access to children after divorce. In addition, women were granted rights to their property after a legal separation or a protection order given as a result of husband's desertion. However, it was not until the Divorce Act 1937 that desertion and insanity became grounds for divorce.

A POSER FOR A BLOOMER.

Old Gentleman. "BEFORE I CAN ENTERTAIN YOUR PROPOSAL, AND GIVE MY CONSENT TO YOUR MARRYING MY SON, I MUST ASK YOU, WHETHER YOU ARE IN A POSITION—A—TO—A—KEEP HIM IN THE STYLE TO WHICH—A—I MAY SAY—HE HAS ALWAYS BEEN ACCUSTOMED? AHEM!"

(Source: www.ntu.ac.uk.)

After the First World War women began to acquire rights, including the right to vote, but they only won them very slowly. It has only been since 1990 that married women have been taxed independently on their own income with their own personal allowance. The right to be paid the same as men for the same work, for example, was only given to women by the Equal Pay Acts 1970 and 1983.

However, employers could still legally discriminate against female workers and the right to be treated equally was granted by the Sex Discrimination Act 1975.

Equal Pay Acts 1970 and 1983

The purpose of the Equal Pay Act 1970 was to end discrimination in pay between men and women. The Act was based upon the concept of 'like work' – this meant that if a man and a woman were doing the same job then they should be on the same pay scale. The problem with the 'like work' concept was that, within a company, men and women often do different tasks. Many work tasks were divided into male jobs and female jobs. Often jobs done primarily by men were graded as more highly skilled and, as a consequence, overall pay discrimination continued. In 1983 the Act was amended to include the concept of 'equal pay for equal value', in other words if a man and a woman have different work tasks but the tasks add equal value to the end product or service, then the people doing the different tasks should be on the same pay scale.

Sex Discrimination Act 1975

The Sex Discrimination Act 1975 established the Equal Opportunities Commission, which would investigate cases of sex discrimination and also campaign for greater gender equality. The 1975 Act made it illegal to discriminate on grounds of sex, and identified a number of different forms of discrimination:

- *Direct discrimination*, which occurs when a person is treated less favourably on grounds of sex.
- *Indirect discrimination*, takes place when a condition must be satisfied in order to obtain a job or promotion, but one sex can satisfy the condition far more easily. The employer has to justify that condition is essential, otherwise indirect discrimination will be said to have taken place.
- *Victimization* is also covered by the Act.

Kingsmill report on women's employment and pay

In April 2001 the British government commissioned Denise Kingsmill to investigate the state of women's employment and pay. Kingsmill consulted the top management of 100 of the UK's leading private and public sector organizations. In December 2001 she published her report, which found an 18 per cent earnings gap between men and women in the UK.

Commenting on the report she said:

> *The Report highlights the demand for better human capital management in the UK. The overwhelming business case for the effective use of the talents and abilities of women offers the greatest potential for reducing the pay gap. My recommendations are aimed at helping organisations to achieve their strategic objectives and develop best practice processes which best serve their needs.*

Her recommendations included:

- Providing more information to staff within organizations through voluntary pay reviews that cover all aspects of women's employment.
- The establishment of a Standards Board to look at the ways in which people are managed at work.
- The commissioning of research on the loss to the economy of failing to make the best use of women's skills in the labour market.
- The use of training tax credits for employers who recruit and train women.
- The introduction of rights of disclosure for individual employees to establish whether they are receiving pay equal to named colleagues.

This is not only an issue in the UK. According to the American Federation of Labor-Congress of Industrial Organizations, around the world, women are more likely than men to hold low-paying jobs.

- In Japan, about 37 per cent of working women hold low-wage jobs compared with only 6 per cent of men.
- In the USA, about 33 per cent of working women hold low-wage jobs compared with 20 per cent of men.
- In the UK, about 31 per cent of working women hold low-wage jobs compared with 13 per cent of men.
- In France, 25 per cent of working women hold low-wage jobs – 8 per cent of men do.
- In Sweden, about 8 per cent of working women hold low-wage jobs – 3 per cent of men do.
- Worldwide, women hold only 14 per cent of administrative and managerial jobs and less than 6 per cent of senior management jobs.

(Source: www.aflcio.org/front/faqs.htm)

What is feminism?

Inspired and radicalized by the events leading up to the French Revolution, Mary Wollstonecraft argued against the forces that kept women ignorant and the superficiality and shallowness they were encouraged to engage in. Mary Wollstonecraft was an early proponent of educational equality between men and women, and her *Vindication of the Rights of Women* (1792) was the first great feminist document. In Paris, where she lived with an American, Gilbert Imlay, during much of the French Revolution, she was close to many of the Revolution's leading political figures.

analyse this

a first-hand account

Read the passage below and attempt the questions that follow:

To account for, and excuse the tyranny of man, many ingenious arguments have been brought forward to prove, that the two sexes, in the acquirement of virtue, ought to aim at attaining a very different character; or, to speak explicitly, women are not allowed to have sufficient strength of mind to acquire what really deserves the name of virtue. Yet it should seem, allowing them to have souls, that there is but one way appointed by Providence to lead mankind to either virtue or happiness.

If then women are not a swarm of ephemeron triflers, why should they be kept in ignorance under the specious name of innocence? Men complain, and with reason, of the follies and caprices of our sex, when they do not keenly satirise our headstrong passions and grovelling vices. Behold, I should answer, the natural effect of ignorance! The mind will ever be unstable that has only prejudices to rest on, and the current will run with destructive fury when there are no barriers to break its force. Women are told from their infancy, and taught by the example of their mothers, that a little knowledge of human weakness, justly termed cunning, softness of temper, outward obedience, and a scrupulous attention to a puerile kind of propriety, will obtain for them the protection of man; and should they be beautiful, everything else is needless, for at least twenty years of their lives.

(Source: Mary Wollstonecraft www.pinn.net/~sunshine/march99/wollstn3.html)

Questions

1. What is Mary Wollstonecraft suggesting is the cause of women's inequality?
2. List the reasons Mary Wollstonecraft gives for women's inequality, and state if you agree or disagree with each reason.
3. Is Mary Wollstonecraft's argument relevant today?

From this initial work of Mary Astell and Mary Wollstonecraft, we saw the emergence of what has become known as *first-wave feminism*, a social movement that focused on obtaining legal and political equality for women. In other words, *first-wave feminism* had the objective of campaigning for a society in which women should be able to do whatever men do. This movement was associated with feminist works such as Simone de Beauvoir's *The Second Sex* (1949), Betty Friedan's *The Feminine Mystique* (1963).

With the introduction of equal pay legislation (1970 and 1983) and equal opportunities legislation (1975) feminist campaigning moved beyond looking at political and legal inequality. A key book in this change to *second-wave feminism* was Kate Millett's *Sexual Politics* (1971). Millett demonstrated that what appeared as *natural* was socially constructed. This argument gave rise to *gynocentric feminism* – recognition that there is a sexual difference that feminists should celebrate.

However, what unites first-wave and second-wave feminism is the use that these feminists make of the concept of patriarchy. This concept is difficult to define, however. Sylvia Walby (1990) has argued that patriarchy exists at two levels of abstraction: at the first level she argues that whenever a man comes into contact with a woman he tries to oppress her and the second level is made up of the six patriarchal structures that Walby defines as:

- Work – women are paid less than men and are less likely to gain promotion because of 'the glass ceiling' – a barrier that women can see beyond but cannot move beyond.
- Family – women are still primarily responsible for housework and childcare; men may *help* but women still have *responsibility.*
- Sexuality – men force women into heterosexual relationships that they neither want nor desire.
- Media – television, newspapers and magazines present images of women as young and attractive, which is an oppressive male gaze.
- Politics – there are very few female MPs and yet MPs make decisions, including making all the legal rules, about all aspects of women's lives, including some of the most intimate things such as age of consent for a sexual relationship, access to contraception and abortion.
- Male violence – in the last analysis men can make use of violence to maintain patriarchy.

Who have the best deal from marriage: women or men?

In 1976 Jesssie Bernard published her influential study *The Future of Marriage* in which she argued that men benefited much more than women from being married. Married men were much more likely to have better health – both physically and mentally – than single men, higher incomes, higher status and generally more successful careers. In contrast, single women are much less likely to suffer ill health and depression than married women. Moreover, single women had more successful careers, higher incomes and more status. Bernard attributed this to the 'Pygmalion effect' – women change their lifestyle and personalities to fit in with their husbands' needs. This was a theme taken up by a number of feminists in the 1980s and 1990s, such as: Hartmann (1981); Chafetz (1990); Lengermann and Niebrugge-Brantley (1990); and Delphy and Leonard (1992) who argued that: 'Within the context of the family system specifically, we see men exploiting women's practical, emotional, sexual and reproductive labour. Loving women does not prevent men from exploiting them' (Delphy and Leonard, 1992, p. 258.)

The argument here is that:

- women still have *responsibility* for housework – men may help but this help is discretionary;
- home is place of leisure for men;
- women provide most of the emotional care within families;
- women are expected to please men and organize their own lives around other members of the family.

However, one of the criticisms of this approach is that feminists have a tendency to express rather than establish the exploitation within marriage. Feminists assume that women cannot redefine the housewife role and exercise power over men.

Ken Dempsey (2002) published a survey of 85 people, both male and female, that asked questions about their perceptions of fairness of the division of labour within the home, childcare, feeling loved, leisure opportunities, and if they were happy with their marriages at the moment. Dempsey found that 75 per cent of tasks performed outside of the home, such as cutting the grass, were performed by men, but 90 per cent of indoor tasks – notably cooking, cleaning – were performed by women. Indoor tasks often took twice as much time to perform and had to be carried out much more often. In addition, women were responsible for childcare in 90 per cent of cases. When asked 'who gets the best deal from marriage?' 78 per cent of women said men got the best deal, whereas 40 per cent of men said they got the best deal. Only 25 per cent of men and 16 per cent of women said that women got the best deal from marriage. When asked to explain the reasons for their answers, one 32-year-old male respondent said: 'Well I say women get the best deal because in a lot of cases they are provided for in a marriage.'

In contrast, women argued that:

They don't have the full responsibility of running a house like we do. They have their job [paid] and their outside jobs at home, but they don't have all the mental stress and worry of the problems to do with the kids and sorting out different things in the household. (47-year-old woman)

Husbands [have the best deal because they] are exempted from responsibility for household chores and jobs to do with the children. (23-year-old woman)

However, some respondents did argue that both men and women did benefit from marriage in different ways:

It is not possible to say because the man gets what he gets from a marriage and a woman gets what she gets. If you're both happy and in love then it's neither gets the better deal. (49-year-old female)

Questions

1. Does the information presented above confirm what you have observed in families that you are familiar with?
2. What explanation do you have for the ways women are treated within marriage?
3. What is your answer to the question: who get the best deal from marriage: women or men? Give reasons for your answer.

When asked about their own marriages, women expressed more dissatisfaction with marriage. Reasons included:

- dissatisfaction with the division of labour;
- childcare responsibilities;
- opportunities for leisure;
- inadequate communication;
- spending insufficient time with partner.

Third-wave feminism

In 1990 Naomi Wolf wrote:

The more legal and material hindrances women have broken through, the more strictly and heavily and cruelly images of female beauty have come to weigh upon us . . . During the past decade, women breached the power

> *structure; meanwhile, eating disorders rose exponentially and cosmetic surgery became the fastest-growing medical speciality . . . It is no accident that so many potentially powerful women feel this way. We are in the midst of a violent backlash against feminism.*

Women are made to feel concern about such things as body shape, hair and other aspects of their physical appearance. The beauty myth is a key element in a powerful backlash against feminism. The ideologies that constitute the myth operate at a psychological and ideological level. Ideas about what constitutes female beauty are used as political weapons to covertly control women, reinforcing the 'glass ceiling' and excluding women from power. Women have a less positive image of their body than men:

- women perceive themselves to be heavier than they are;
- women are more concerned about their body attractiveness than men;
- women are less satisfied with their body than men;
- women are more dissatisfied with some aspect of their appearance – and this includes not only mature women but children as young as six years of age;
- for women body image has a significant effect upon psychological health, romantic relationships and femininity.

In contrast, Camille Paglia is highly critical of Naomi Wolf, and many other second- and third-wave feminists. Paglia's argument draws upon Hobbes, Sade and Nietzsche to show that the feminist project of undermining patriarchy is damaging to civilization and will cause great hurt and pain to us all if it is successful.

analyse this

influences on Paglia

Marquis de Sade (1740–1814)

Sade is widely regarded as a gruesome transgressor who used his fanatical ideas to lead a truly scandalous life. In his novels, he theorized about the thrill of torture. Sade believed that both sexual deviation and criminal acts are natural. He used this belief to justify extremely degrading sexual experiences in which extreme violence and other cruelty was inflicted to attain sexual pleasure. In the nineteenth century Richard von Krafft-Ebing took Sade's name to describe a form of sexual perversion involving the infliction of pain (*sadism*).

Thomas Hobbes (1588–1679)

Hobbes' philosophy as outlined in *The Leviathan* (1651) assumes that human nature is essentially 'animal' and dominated by self interest, which leads directly to an endless state of war between all individuals. In this state of nature life becomes 'solitary, poor, nasty, brutish, and short'. To avoid this condition, Hobbes argued, that we should form a commonwealth, in which individuals place absolute sovereign power in the hands of a strong ruler. For Hobbes, this obedience to strong government is necessary in order to have control over our animal instincts, secure liberty and allow us to have respect for others.

Friedrich Nietzsche (1844–1900)

For Nietzsche morality, including ideas or 'good' and 'evil', are imposed upon us by people who have *the will to power* – the powerful invent both god and religion to control the behaviour of others. Nietzsche's philosophy is a philosophy of 'becoming' in which the person should be free to lead their life as they wish and 'become' whatever they wish. Nietzsche allows us to think beyond the limits of moral obligation and what he would see as the fictitious demands of an imaginary god. For Nietzsche we should attempt to overcome external constraints on our behaviour by becoming *Übermensch* or 'Overman' (often referred to as 'Superman'), a person who attempts to rise up and overcome the imposition of morality and sanctions of others (the will to power) and prevent us from exercising our freedom.

As we shall see below, Camille Paglia brings these three sets of philosophical ideas about morality, power, violence and human nature together to inform her analysis of gender issues.

For Paglia people are animals; they are part of nature and in a state of nature life is nasty, brutish and short. Nature has a history for Paglia, which is a history of people attempting to control nature's power. Social organization is an artificial creation, built as a defence against nature's power. Sexual power takes the form of Nietzsche's 'will to power' and this force is contained by Hobbesian social arrangements for strong government, as found in the Commonwealth. As she later very forcefully explains: 'It is nature, not society, that is our greatest oppressor.' She adds: 'Society is not the enemy, as feminism ignorantly claims. Society is woman's protection against rape.'

Questions

1. Wolf argues that there is a link between female liberation and female beauty. Do you accept or reject this argument? State the reasons for your answer.
2. In *Sexual Personae* (1990) Camille Paglia wrote: 'If civilization had been left in female hands, we would still be living in grass huts.' Do you accept or reject this statement? Give three reasons for your answer. Do you agree with Camille Paglia that the feminist project of undermining patriarchy is damaging to civilization and will cause great hurt and pain to us all if it were to be successful?
3. 'Women have the same legal, political and social rights as men.' If this is the case do we still need feminism?
4. Does the evidence of discrimination against women mean that Britain needs a Bill of Rights?
5. What gender rights should be written into a Bill of Rights? Who would stand in judgment on them?

2

Class and inequality

We live in societies where the distribution of power, wealth and prestige is unequal. Individuals can be placed into different strata on the basis of:

- the number and quality of their possessions, such as houses, cars and fine clothes, commonly known as *wealth*;
- their ability to make people do what they want them to do, commonly known as *power*;
- the respect, standing or status that they each enjoy within their community, commonly known as *prestige*.

For most social scientists, differences in the distribution of power, wealth and prestige form the basis of social class. A number of researchers have argued that social class and, in particular, poverty and exclusion are the most important factors determining our life chances. It is argued that social class helps to determine a person's level of educational attainment, number of years of life, chances of getting a serious disease or suffering a serious injury at work, as well as having a determining effect upon our cultural tastes and leisure patterns. In this chapter we shall look at some of the contrasting theories of class and ask a few questions about whether we still live in 'class societies', the advantages of equality and inequality, whether it is possible to move from one class to another, and whether there are other ways of dividing people up into strata that have more of an impact on person's life – such as division according to race or gender.

The analysis of class is often associated with the nineteenth-century political economist Karl Marx (1818–83). Since the collapse of communism in eastern Europe, few social scientists believe that Marx has anything valid to say about the current state of either the economy or the wider society. However, it would be wrong to dismiss the Marxian analysis totally. In the nineteenth century Marx and Engels constructed a philosophy of history that singled out class divisions as the motor of history – the factor that pushed history forwards.

For Marx there were two significant classes in capitalist societies such as ours in which companies run to make a profit for their owners:

- the *bourgeoisie* – the class that owns the factories, shops and offices;
- the *proletariat* – the class of people who do not own the factories, shops and offices.

From the Marxian perspective, the group that owns the factories, shops and offices – which Marx referred to as the means of production – not only has economic power, it also has political power. According to the Marxian analysis the bourgeoisie exploit the proletariat by not paying them the full value of their labour power. In other words, workers are only paid a fraction of the profits that they generate for the bourgeoisie. The state is viewed as an institution that helps to organize capitalist society in the best interests of the bourgeoisie. Moreover, working-class people are said to hold values, ideas and beliefs about the nature of inequality that it is not in their own economic interests to hold. Working-class people have their ideas manipulated by the media, schools and religion, for example, and regard economic inequality as fair and just. Marxists refer to this manipulation of the ideas of working class as *ideological* – working-class people are said to be victims of a *false consciousness.*

Marx also recognized the inventiveness that flourished under capitalism: the railway, the electric telegraph, the application of chemistry to both industry and agriculture, and steam navigation were all discussed by Marx in positive terms. However, capitalism brings with it inequality, exploitation and alienation. The bourgeoisie, the capitalist class who own the means of production, can only make a profit if they do not pay their workers (the proletariat) the true value of their labour power. It was upon this premise that Marx developed the 'labour theory of value'. In addition, for Marx, individual people are essentially creative beings; to make things is the key element of our *species being,* Marx argued. However, within capitalism work is dull, boring and monotonous and does not give people opportunity to express their creativeness. This inability to express creativity is what Marx termed *alienation.* Within capitalism workers are made to feel that they are merely part of the machine.

At the turn of the twentieth century a sociologist named Max Weber argued for an alternative view of class, which contrasted with Marx's. In addition to the bourgeoisie, Weber said that the people who own large amounts of land – whom he named the *rentier class* – also had significant power. Moreover, the classes that did not own property could themselves be divided into different classes on the basis of the level of skill that they had and the demand for that skill in the market place. If a skill is in short supply, in other words if only a few people have a particular ability and there is a big demand for that skill or ability, then such people will be in a position to demand high financial rewards. In a similar fashion, if people have few skills, or skills that are easily acquired, then such people are not in a position to demand high financial rewards. For Weber, a social class is a group of people who share the same class position! By this Weber meant that a social class is made up of a group of people who have similar:

- market situation – they earn a similar amount of money;
- work situation – they have similar conditions of service at work.

However, for Weber, social class was only one aspect of a person's *stratification position*. Other aspects of how people are divided into strata are:

- *status*, which Weber defined as the social estimation of honour;
- *party*, which Weber defined as the amount of political power that a person had.

Status, in the Weberian analysis, is what people think of a person in terms of the amount of prestige that the person has. Weber argued that status was independent of both social class and party – in other words, people can have a high social class position but this does not guarantee that they will have a high status position. Similarly, a person may have low social class position but high status. Moreover, in contrast to Marx, Weber thought that the people who hold political power can come from any social class and may or may not have a high status.

In 1973 Anthony Giddens put forward an alternative view of what he termed *class structuration*. Unlike the models of class suggested by Marx and Weber, Giddens argued that individual people *create* social class through a process of *structuration*. For Giddens there are two forms of class structuration: mediate structuration and proximate structuration.

Mediate structuration is concerned with the ways in which class advantages are passed on from one generation to the next. Parents love their children and want them to be successful in life; children from professional middle-class families are given greater access to additional skills, abilities and resources. Middle-class children may be informally taught to be more articulate by their parents. The additional language skills can be used as a resource by children in schools, helping them to gain qualifications to obtain professional middle-class occupations.

Proximate structuration has three elements to it:

- Division of labour – we look up to certain occupations such as the older, traditional occupations like doctors, barristers and solicitors or alternatively high-profile celebrities such as professional footballers or pop stars. Similarly, there are occupations that we look down upon. If our estimations are commonly shared and accepted by the people in those occupations, this helps to reproduce a hierarchy of occupations, or social class hierarchy.

- Authority – in any place of work there are people who give orders and people who do as they are told. If you are given an instruction at your place of work and carry it out because you believe that the person giving you the instruction has a right to do so, again this helps to reinforce the social class hierarchy.
- Distributive groupings – unlike Marx and Weber, Giddens thought that 'consumption' also has a role to play in the process of structuration. The type of house you live in, the area of the town or city where it is located, where you shop, what car you drive, the clothes you wear and the logos you display are all significant. If others see your patterns of consumption as 'better', then this helps to reinforce the class hierarchy.

However, in the 1990s Giddens changed his mind about class and argued that class divisions were no longer significant in determining people's life chances. In *Beyond Right and Left* (1994) he argued that:

- Class is no longer experienced as 'class', but as a series of individual constraints and opportunities.
- Some professional people and other high-income earners, attempt to exclude themselves from the wider society by not making use of the NHS or state schools and living in houses or apartments that are patrolled by guards.
- Lifestyle and taste have become significant as markers of social differentiation. The 'generational transmission belt' of class is broken; parents have much less importance in determining the life chances of their children.
- Class is no longer a 'lifetime experience' because of global influences upon the economy, movement up and down the class ladder affect everybody.
- The only significant 'class' division within the population is between the people who are employed and the new poor who have become excluded from the labour market.

Some people, such as Malcolm Waters (1997), have suggested that the stratification system is moving away from a class-based economic system to a culturalist or status-conventional phase. He argues that the status-conventional phase is based upon the following four social changes, which we take into account when we try to place somebody in a stratification system:

- culturalism – a greater emphasis on lifestyle choices, aesthetic preferences and value commitments;

key term

poverty

According to Peter Townsend (1979) poverty is a condition where a person has insufficient resources, such as cash and capital as-sets, to enjoy a *style of life* that the rest of us take for granted. People in poverty are unable to participate in activities such as buying a warm winter coat during cold weather, or buying a friend a birthday card.

key terms

primary poverty

When income falls below the minimum required because of:

- death of the chief wage earner;
- incapacity of chief wage earner because of accident, illness or old age;
- chief wage earner out of work;
- chronic irregularity of work;
- large family;
- low wage.

- fragmentation – constantly changing associations between people;
- autonomization – greater irrationality experienced in our everyday lives;
- resignification – a constant reflection on interests, choices and emotions in which we are concerned about how we present ourselves.

For Waters, 'occupation' is little more than a badge or the consumption status that we have.

The poor, the excluded, the underclass

Absolute poverty is where people are destitute, living on the streets and are so lacking in resources that they may die. A condition of absolute poverty does exist in many of the world's poorer countries. As the economist A.K. Sen stated in 1982: 'While it can hardly be denied that malnutrition captures only one aspect of our idea of poverty, it is an important aspect, and one that is particularly important for many developing countries. It seems clear that malnutrition must have a central place in the conception of poverty.'

Townsend, however, is discussing the notion of *relative poverty.* A number of people have criticized this conception of poverty because it involves looking a the lifestyle of affluent people and claiming people are *poor* if they cannot afford to live in the same way as affluent people. In other words, Townsend is not talking about *poverty*, but inequality. As Dr Rhodes Boyson suggested when he was Minister for Social Security in the 1980s: 'Those on the poverty line in the United States earn more than 50 times the average income of someone in India. That is what relative poverty is all about . . . Apparently, the more people earn, the more they believe poverty exists, presumably so that they can be pleased about the fact it is not themselves who are poor' (*Hansard*, 28 June 1984).

The study of poverty has a long history in the social sciences. Drawing upon the language of exclusion, William Booth (1890) in his book *Darkest England and the Way Out* used 'black Africa' as a simile for 'dark England' and described the poor as 'tribes of savages'. George Sims (1883) in his book *How the Poor Live* describes a 'dark continent that is within easy walking distance of the General Post Office . . . the wild races who inhabit it will, I trust, gain public sympathy as easily as [other] savage tribes.' Henry Mayhew (1861) in 'London Labour and London Poor' described the poor as London's 'wandering tribes of bushmen'.

secondary poverty

According to Rowntree in 1901, secondary poverty occurs when people are unable to meet their minimum requirements because of: 'drink, betting and gambling. Ignorant or careless housekeeping, and other improvident expenditure, the latter often induced by irregularity of income.'

However, it was Seebohm Rowntree (1901) who did the first systematic study of the poverty of poor people in the city of York. Based upon scientific evidence from researchers who had done work on prisoners in Scotland to find the minimum nutritional requirement for a person to live, Rowntree identified the amount of money needed to satisfy the basic food, clothing and housing needs, and he gave this a price. A family was said to be in poverty if its income fell below this level.

Rowntree made a distinction between the *deserving* and the *undeserving* poor, which has had a lasting impact upon social policy to this day. The Beveridge Report (1942) was based upon Rowntree's research, and the Beveridge Plan was the foundation for the post-1945 Welfare State. The Beveridge Plan aimed to create a comprehensive and universal welfare state that would address the five giant problems of:

- disease;
- ignorance;
- squalor;
- idleness;
- want.

However, during the Thatcher years from 1975 to 1990, the aim of the government was to generate an 'enterprise culture' in Britain.

analyse this

is poverty a bad thing?

The information and arguments that we have looked at so far assume that poverty is a bad thing, but the poor have a number of important functions to perform for the wider society.

Look at the list of points drawn from the work of Herbert Gans (1973) – do you accept or reject his arguments? Explain your answers.

1. Poverty helps to ensure that dirty and dangerous jobs get done.
2. The poor save the rich money by providing cheap services, such as domestic servants.
3. The poor provide employment for the army, police and social workers.
4. The poor buy the stale and damaged goods.
5. The poor provide emotional satisfaction for the rich, by evoking compassion.
6. The poor help to promote middle-class values by being lazy and spendthrift.
7. The poor fail at school and help to legitimize the success of the non-poor.

The deprivation index

In his study of poverty Townsend attempted to define the 'style of living' of people in Britain and identify the percentage of people who were unable to afford the lifestyle that Townsend believed we all take for granted. He used the deprivation index to measure poverty.

Below is the list of characteristics that according to Peter Townsend represents the 'style of living' in the UK, followed by the percentage number of people in the population who are 'deprived' on the basis of each characteristic.

1. Has not had a week's holiday away from home in last 12 months (53.6 per cent).
2. (For adults only.) Has not had a relative or friend to the home for a meal or snack in the last four weeks (33.4 per cent).
3. (Adults only.) Has not been out in the last four weeks to a relative or friend for a meal or snack (45.1 per cent).
4. (Children only (under 15). Has not had a friend to play or to tea in the last four weeks (36.3 per cent).
5. (Children only.) Did not have a party on last birthday (56.6 per cent).
6. Has not had an afternoon or evening out for entertainment in the last two weeks (47 per cent).
7. Does not have fresh meat (including meals out) as many as four days a week (19.3 per cent).
8. Has gone through one or more days in the past fortnight without a cooked meal (7 per cent).
9. Has not had a cooked breakfast most days of the week (67.3 per cent).
10. Household does not have a refrigerator (45.1 per cent).
11. Household does not usually have a Sunday joint (three out of four times) (25.9 per cent).
12. Household does not have sole use of four amenities indoors (flush WC; sink or washbasin and cold-water tap; fixed bath or shower; and gas or electric cooker) (21.4 per cent).

Do you accept or reject the deprivation index as an effective measure of poverty? Give the reasons for your answer.

Piachaud (1981) pointed out that:

> *To choose not to go on holiday or eat meat is one thing: it may interest sociologists, but is of no interest to those concerned with poverty. To have little or no opportunity to take a holiday or buy meat is entirely different.*

What Piachaud is suggesting here is that Townsend's deprivation index does not take choice into account. I might choose not to have breakfast, not to invite friends round and not to go out for the evening, but this does not mean that I am poor. Townsend has taken his own definition of what a style of life should be like and has assumed that people who do not follow it must be poor.

Thatcherism

Under the leadership of Mrs Thatcher the Conservatives became closely associated with 'New Right' ideas. These included:

- an emphasis on personal liberty and personal freedom;
- the free market and opposition to state planning;
- popular capitalism – notably privatization and home ownership;
- the promotion of the 'normal' heterosexual family;
- reduction of public spending;
- giving people incentives to work by lowering both taxes and benefits;
- making people less dependent upon the welfare state.

At the level of rhetoric, Thatcherism was seen as conviction politics, as enterprise culture pushing back the 'nanny state'. For New Right thinkers the welfare state removed freedom and responsibility, reduced incentives, produced waste, promoted social grievances and removed individual freedom. In other words, the welfare state produced a dangerous underclass.

In many respects this was because, from a Thatcherite perspective, unemployment was blamed upon the unemployed themselves; they had priced themselves out of jobs by demanding higher wages.

In sharp contrast to much post-1945 social policy, the New Right argued that the welfare state was damaging to the wider economy and society. The welfare state took away the incentive to work for people by providing over-generous benefits and imposing high taxes. In other words, people were poor not because of factors outside of their control but because the welfare state had made them lazy. The welfare state was said to have created a 'dependency culture' – what academics would call a 'culture of poverty'.

Culture of poverty

In the 1960s Oscar Lewis wrote a number of books such as *The Children of Sanchez* (1965) and *La Vida* (1968) in which he argued that the poor form an underclass, or subgroup in society, with their own set of self-defeating values, which are passed on from one generation to the next:

- At an individual level, poor people have strong feelings of marginality, helplessness and inadequacy.
- At the family level, parents pass on such feelings to children.
- This is reinforced at a community level, where whole communities passively accept the situation that they are in and people are discouraged from bettering themselves or their families.

According to Lewis it is possible to identify the same features in poor communities in large cities across North and South America and in Europe:

- unemployment and under-employment;
- the people are unskilled;
- high levels of child labour;
- little or no savings;
- no food reserves in the home;
- only buying small amounts of food if and when the need arises;
- pawning personal possessions;
- borrowing from local money lenders at very high rates of interest;
- buying second-hand clothes and furniture.

The poor have a set of social and psychological characteristics that make them different from other people in society and are the most important factor in keeping the poor in the situation they are in. Lewis lists these characteristics as:

- no respect for privacy;
- gregariousness;
- alcoholism;
- regular use of violence to settle differences of opinion;
- regular use of violence in the upbringing of children;
- wife beating;
- early introduction into sexual relationships;
- living together;
- high incidence of the abandonment of mothers and children, together with a martyr complex amongst women who enjoyed outlining how bad the men in their lives were;
- little planning for the future.

In 1986 the government made significant changes to the social security system in an effort to encourage self-reliance and independence. These changes included the introduction of income support, a means-tested benefit for people who had not made sufficient National Insurance contributions to receive unemployment benefit ('jobseekers allowance'). A means-tested benefit is a benefit that can only be received if applicants can demonstrate that they are in genuine need. 'Family credit' was also introduced for low-income families in work – this was another means-tested benefit. The introduction of the social fund, a cash-limited fund of money that people on benefit can draw upon to cover the cost of things they require such as cookers. In most cases the money from the social fund is a loan, which must be paid back.

There are a number of criticisms of the 'culture of poverty' argument. Firstly, it appears to be based upon a set of middle-class values. Secondly, Oscar Lewis did not gather statistical evidence but relied upon his own observations of families. Thirdly, the boundaries between the poor and the rest of society are not clearly identified. Fourth, some of the values he identifies as part of the culture of the poor are found in other classes.

There was an interesting change in our attitude to welfare between 1945 and 1986. As Zygmunt Bauman (1997) explained, in 1945 people tended to see welfare as something which was owned by the community and given back to the community in times of need; by 1986, however, welfare was seen as something that 'we' give to 'others' and that the nation can no longer afford.

analyse this

Peter Townsend has suggested a policy for an 'effective assault' on poverty in Britain that involves:

- abolition of excessive wealth;
- abolition of excessive income;
- introduction of an equitable income structure and some breaking down of the distinction between earners and dependants;
- abolition of unemployment;
- reorganization of employment and professional practice – more industrial democracy;
- reorganization of community service;
- abolish the distinction between owner-occupiers and tenants.

Questions

1 Explain if you support the policy that Townsend is putting forward to end poverty.

2 What do you think are the differences between poverty and inequality? Outline the reasons for your answer. Do you think that the significance of social class has declined?

3

Citizenship and race

On 22 April 1993, black teenager Stephen Lawrence was murdered in south-east London. The way in which the police handled the investigation raised the issue of whether there was institutional racism within the police force. In July 1997 the government asked Sir William Macpherson to investigate what lessons should be learned about police investigation and prosecution of racially motivated crimes in general. When the Macpherson Report was published in February 1999 it made 70 recommendations on how to break down institutionalized racism. The report also raised the important issue of the links between citizenship rights and race.

In 2000 the government revised the Race Relations Act 1976 in response to the recommendations made by the Stephen Lawrence Inquiry Report, the Commission for Racial Equality (CRE) review of the workings of the 1976 Act and the European Union Directive 2000/43/EC. This European Union Directive (2000/43/EC) established, for the first time in Europe, the principle of racial equality between persons within the European Union, a minimum standard of legal protection against racism. The Act makes both direct racial discrimination and indirect racial discrimination illegal:

- *direct racial discrimination* – when a person is treated less favourably on racial grounds, that is on grounds of colour, race, ethnic origin or nationality;
- *indirect racial discrimination* – where treatment is formally equal, but has discriminatory consequences.

The Race Relations Act 2000 gives the police, local councils, tax inspectors and other public bodies the duty to eliminate racial discrimination and promote equality of opportunity. In addition, the CRE has the power to issue a *compliance notice* to any public body whom it believes is not providing good relations between racial groups. Chief police officers are *vicariously liable* for acts of racial discrimination by police officers.

The 2000 Act redefines the role of the CRE. The duties of the CRE are now:

- to move towards the elimination of racial discrimination;
- to promote equality of opportunity;
- to promote good relations between racial groups;
- to review the effectiveness of the race relations legislation and suggest amendments to the government;
- to conduct formal investigations into cases of alleged racial discrimination.

What is citizenship?

It is commonly assumed that youth crime is increasing dramatically and something needs to be done about young people because they are out of control. Many older people's opinions of the young today are that they are lacking in morality and ambition, they are lazy, not wanting to work, not courteous, have poor manners, are dangerous and are in serious need of *remoralization*.

Similar opinions have been expressed in the press. The *Daily Mail* (28 April 2002) described young people today as 'a terrifying generation of murderous, morally blank wolf-children, fatherless, undisciplined, indulged one minute then brutalised the next'. It expressed the view (30 April 2002) that, 'As we go around the country and talk to people, there seems no issue that matters more to people than anti-social behaviour and street crime.'

Lynda Lee-Potter, also writing in the *Mail*, argued that: 'Too many children have no education, discipline, supportive families, a structure to their lives and future.' These factors all lead to trouble, which results in children 'knowing about their rights but not their responsibilities.' Lynda Lee-Potter concludes by observing that 'unless we face the truth, increasing generations of no-hopers will be born and they too, will be victims destined for brutal lives' (*Daily Mail*, 1 May 2002).

The idea that 'something needs to be done about out-of-control young people' also underpins much government policy. David Blunkett was reported in the *Guardian* (14 December 2001) saying: 'this week's reports show that too many of our towns and cities lack any sense of civic identity or shared values. The tradition of political citizenship in the UK is so weak that to raise the issue of what unites us is deemed marginal at best, dishonest at worst.'

Citizenship education is one of the ways in which young people can be taught duties and responsibilities. In 2002 the government published a Green Paper on education for those between the ages of 14 and 19 (*14–19: Extending Opportunities, Raising Standards*) in which it said: 'Post-16 Citizenship should enable young adults to exercise social responsibility and extend their potential effectiveness by active participation in their education and training and their communities.'

Citizenship classes should include how to take part in democracy and how to express themselves; they should make young people aware of current events and ready to debate issues, including some basics of how laws are made and who declares war. As Sir Bernard Crick has argued: 'Citizenship is a necessary condition for a more participatory society.'

Moreover, as the *Guardian* argued (14 December 2001): 'it is vital that we develop a stronger understanding of what our collective citizenship means, and how we can build a shared commitment into our social and political institutions.' However, the original report on *Education for Citizenship and the Teaching of Democracy in Schools* warned that: 'Schools can only do so much . . . we must not ask too little of teachers but equally we must not ask too much. Pupil's attitudes to active citizenship are influenced quite as much by . . . many factors other than schooling: by family, the immediate environment, the media and the examples of those in public life. Sometimes these are positive factors, sometimes not.'

The *Guardian* (14 December 2001) argued that: 'Citizenship means finding a common place for diverse cultures and beliefs, consistent with our core values.' Different cultures have their beliefs but they still need to meet the needs of common values in British society. David Blunkett has suggested that asylum seekers should take a form of citizenship test, together with an English test, and swear an oath of allegiance to Britain. These measures should enhance our sense of citizenship, which the government appears to believe brings together society.

key term

British citizenship

This is citizenship for people closely connected with the UK, including the Channel Islands and the Isle of Man. British citizens have the right to live here permanently and are free to leave and re-enter the UK at any time. (Source: www.britain.org.nz/vpass/britcit.html.)

Citizenship can be seen as a relationship between the state and the individual and at the same time political relationships between individuals. There are four main perspectives on the nature of citizenship: social liberalism, neo-liberalism, communitarianism, and civic-republicanism.

Social liberalism

Taking their starting point from John Lock's *Treatises of Government* (1690), which argued that men had a natural right to life, liberty and property, citizenship is seen to be both universal and equal. Social liberalism is the most influential theory of citizenship in Europe and North America. This perspective assumes a rather passive form of citizenship in which all people born within a given nation state are citizens of that nation state and, as such, are given a number of formal legal and political rights, duties and responsibilities.

Other assumptions include:

- All men can think, therefore all men are equal.
- Individualism – if individuals make a mistake this is unfortunate for that individual and their immediate family or friends. However, if a strong and powerful government makes a mistake then many people suffer.

John Rawls

Rawls discusses the notion of citizenship within the context of a wider discussion of justice. He makes a distinction between the public sphere and the private sphere. In the public sphere, social and political institutions should be based upon principles of justice:

- all people should have equal rights guaranteed by a system of basic liberties;
- the system of equal rights helps to secure self respect;
- people are free from coercion;
- participation in politics is a right, not an obligation;
- social and economic inequality should emerge from an open competition between people, and be based upon equality of opportunity.

T.H. Marshall

The debate about the social liberal conception of citizenship usually takes its starting point from the sociologist T.H. Marshall. For Marshall there are three types of citizenship rights:

- *civil rights or our legal citizenship* – rights associated with individual freedom, such as the right to free speech, to own property, equality before the law;
- *political rights* – rights associated with democracy, such as the right to vote;
- *social rights* – mainly our welfare rights, such as the right to education, health care and social security. The philosophy that underpinned the welfare state.

In 1964 Marshall wrote:

> *citizenship is a status bestowed on those who are full members of a community. All who possess the status are equal with respect to the rights and duties with which the status is endowed.*

Critiques of Marshall

- First, Marshall's notion of citizenship is 'incomplete' in that he did not regard control over the workplace by the citizen as significant. In other words, Marshall had no conception of 'economic citizenship' based upon industrial democracy.
- Second, Marshall did not take into account 'cultural rights'. In the early part of the twentieth century many governments attempted to suppress minority languages, making people speak the majority language.
- In the latter part of the century, there was a rise in the notion of multiculturalism and a growing recognition that people should not be restricted in their choice of language, religion or other cultural practices.
- Marshall's work has been criticized by feminists on the grounds that it is built upon assumptions that men go out to work and women stay at home doing domestic work.
- Marshall also naively assumed that the citizenship rights that we enjoy are both evolutionary and cumulative – that once an individual had won a civil or political right it could not be taken away.
- Marshall had a one-dimensional view of citizenship; he had no division between an active citizen and a passive citizen.
- Some forms of citizenship, such as those that emerged from the French Revolution, were based upon the active involvement in social and political struggle, Marshall's conception of citizenship is passive. The citizen is a passive person who receives a range of benefits from the state.

Turner (1999) argues that an adequate understanding of the problems surrounding issues of citizenship in contemporary societies must go well beyond Marshall's framework. T.H. Marshall attempted to create a form of citizenship that took into account the two contradictory principles of scarcity and the need for solidarity:

- he defined citizenship as a collection of rights that provided the individual with a formal legal identity;
- however, at the same time 'citizenship' institutions control the access of individuals to scarce resources, who gets social security, health care, housing, and so forth;
- citizenship not only provides criteria for inclusion and exclusion of people from the wider society; it provides the foundation for a cultural and political identity.

We have moved from a discussion of inclusion and exclusion in relation to class advantages to struggles about sexual identity, gay rights, asylum seeking, residence and criteria for membership of a political community.

Active forms of citizenship

Bruce Ackerman: the dialogic theory of liberal legitimacy

Bruce Ackerman's *Social Justice in the Liberal State* (1980) argues that we live in a world of scarce resources and struggle in which we constantly have to justify our claim for resources. Ackerman rejects the central assumptions of social contract theorists; rather, he assumes that people have no rights except for those that they acquire through their constant interaction with others who may be making claims for our resources. As Ackerman explains:

> *Rather than linking liberalism to ideas of natural right or imaginary contract,* we must learn to think of liberalism as a way of talking about power, a form of political culture . . . *If there is anything distinctive about liberalism, it must be in the* kinds of reasons *liberals rely on to legitimate their claims to scarce resources. Nazis are not liberals because there is* something *about the reasons they give in support of their claims that is inconsistent with the organizing principles of liberal power talk.* (author's emphasis.)

The conditions that Ackerman proposes include:

- for the justification of power to be legitimate it must be intelligible and consistent;
- claims to power must be neutral; power claims that depend upon one person claiming to be a moral authority are illegitimate in a liberal society. In other words, any claim to legitimacy that depends upon one person claiming to be intrinsically superior to fellow citizens should be rejected.

Ackerman makes a distinction between *manna* – an imaginary resource that can be transformed into any material object in the world – and the citizen. A stone can be *manna* but cannot be a citizen, although we might give stones some rights and protection, as we do with the Grand Canyon. Areas of natural beauty can be given the right to our protection but this does not make them citizens. A lion is *manna* but not a citizen, even though it has some communicative competence and can roar its dissatisfaction. *Manna* does not pass what Ackerman calls the *dialogic test for citizenship:* 'a liberal relationship is defined as a social condition in which power wielders ask and answer each others' questions of legitimacy'.

The liberal state as a political system, according to Ackerman, is nothing more than a collection of individuals who can participate in a dialogue in which all aspects of their power position may be justified in a certain way. The political system is constituted by this process of dialogic interchange. Moreover, any individual who wishes to be classified as a citizen must be able to fulfil a minimum dialogic competence. This minimum dialogic competence for citizenship involves firstly the ability to pass the *defensive test*, which is the ability to say 'because I am at least as good as you are'. And secondly a person must pass the inquiry test which is the ability to say 'why should you get it rather than I?'

Finally, Ackerman argues that there is a *behavioural condition for citizenship* that is broken if you attempt to deprive people of their rights to material subsistence if that person has done nothing to deprive you of yours.

For Ackerman, active participation in dialogue is central to the notion of citizenship. It is by such exchanges of dialogue that power and legitimacy are established, the rules by which the political system are established and maintained, and by which our freedom and vision of the good life is established and maintained.

However, not all people are classified as 'citizens'. Who should be included as a *citizen* and who should be excluded?

analyse this

racial classification

Racial classification has a central role to play in any discussion of citizenship. In 1997 Richard Dyer published his book *White* in which he argued that 'race' is something that is only applied to non-white people. Race may be about the biological classification of people on the basis of the differences that can be observed, notably skin colour. However, for Dyer being a white person and viewing oneself as 'human' rather than 'raced' helps to secure a position of power for whiter people. 'Other' people are 'raced' but white people are 'just people', as he explains:

> *There is no more powerful position than being 'just' human. The claim to power is the claim to speak for the commonality of humanity. Raced people can't do that – they can only speak for their race. But non-raced people can, for they do not represent the interests of a race.*

Questions

1. What does it mean to be a *white* person?
2. If you are a white person, do you feel that you belong to a race?

British nationality

In 1981 the British government passed the British Nationality Act, which legally defined who was entitled to be classified as a British citizen. The Act established three separate forms of citizenship:

- British citizenship – people who were born in the UK or who had a parent born in the UK;
- British-dependent territories citizens – people who were born or are resident in a British-dependent territory;
- British overseas citizenship – people who were born or are resident in one of the following places:

- Anguilla
- Bermuda
- British Antarctic Territory
- British Indian Ocean Territory
- British Virgin Islands
- Cayman Islands
- Falkland Islands
- Gibraltar
- Montserrat
- Pitcairn Islands
- St Helena
- Ascension Island
- Tristan Da Cunha
- South Georgia and the South Sandwich Islands
- Turks and Caicos Islands

The latter two groups – British-dependent territories citizens and the British overseas citizens – effectively lost British citizenship because they were no longer allowed to permanently live and work in the UK.

analyse this

a history of deceit

The following was written by the Anguilla Independence Movement:

Since 1962 the consistent intention of British politics has been to keep Black and Asian people out of Britain. The start of modern legislation dealing with nationality issues was the 1962 Immigration Act. The 1948 Nationality Act gave all British subjects the right of admission to the UK. It represented the first time that immigration controls had been applied against Commonwealth citizens. In practice, White Commonwealth citizens were not subject to controls while Black Commonwealth citizens had now to apply for work vouchers.

In 1965 the Labour party government published a White Paper, entitled 'Immigration from the Commonwealth' it significantly reduced the number of work vouchers.

The 1968 Commonwealth Immigrants Act introduced by the Labour party revealed once again that the dividing line for admission to Britain was race. This Act allowed entry to Britain only if a person, or one parent or grandparent was born or naturalised in the UK, this Act was aimed at Asians living in the newly independent African countries, for example White settlers from Kenya holding British passports was welcomed while Asians also holding British passports were excluded.

The Conservative party in their 1971 Immigration Act took the Labour party's idea in the 1968 Act of 'birth and ancestry' one step further. The new terms of 'Patrial' and 'non-Patrial' were introduced for the first time in this Act. For the first time there was a clear distinction between white and non-white Citizens of the UK and Colonies. The whites called Patrials had the absolute right of entry; non-Patrials were subject to immigration control. Entry into the UK required a direct link of descent by blood. The vast majority of non-whites could not meet this requirement. The 1971 Act came into force on 1 January 1973, the very date Britain joined the EEC. This proved the fallacy in their arguments, at the very point Britain was using a variety immigration controls to actively close its door on non-white people from the Commonwealth, it was opening its borders to nationals of European countries.

It was the 1981 British Nationality Act that abolished the term 'patriality' and replaced it with the new term: those with a 'close connection' with Britain. Although this term meant exactly the same as 'patriality' it was changed because of criticism from the European Human Rights Commission that had described UK immigration law as racially motivated and degrading. The 1981 Nationality Act introduced five categories of British nationals – British citizens, British Dependent Territories citizens, British Overseas citizens, British Protected Persons and British subjects. It is important to note that only the first category carries the right of abode in the UK. The other four categories carry no such right and are nothing more than worthless forms of nationality. The Conservative party introduced another Immigration Act in 1988. This new Act repealed Section 1 (5) of the 1971 Act, which had assured Commonwealth citizens, settled in the UK before 1 January 1973 that wives and children would have freedom to enter the UK. In consistent British hypocrisy the 1988 Act reassured white Commonwealth citizens with ancestral links to UK and EEC nationals that their existing rights to family life would continue. Again Britain opened its doors to white immigrants and their families while putting every possible restriction on the entry of non-white people and their families. One method used against non-whites was the interviews at overseas posts and the method of questioning. Questions were clearly designed not to get the truth but to find reasons for refusal.

The purpose of law, according to Martin Luther King, is to establish justice. A just law upholds human dignity while an unjust law undermines it. Anguillians must learn the difference between laws that are just and laws that are unjust. Laws that sanction racism can never be just. Laws based on racism can have no place in a democratic society.

24th September 2001

(Source: www.anguillanews.com/Anguillanews/submission3.html)

Questions

1 Do you accept or reject the view expressed in the passage that: 'Since 1962 the consistent intention of British politics has been to keep Black and Asian people out of Britain'? Give reasons for your answer.

2 In your own words explain what you believe is the meaning of the sentence in the passage that states: 'A just law upholds human dignity while an unjust law undermines it.'

Asylum seekers and refugees

Although the British government has a fairly narrow view of who is a British citizen, the government argues that it has a good record on providing a safe haven for asylum seekers and refugees. In 1951 the government signed the UN Convention on Refugees. The Convention stated that a refugee is a person who has a:

well-founded fear of being persecuted for reasons of race, religion, nationality, membership of a particular social group, or political opinion, is outside the country of his nationality, and is unable or, owing to such fear, is unwilling to avail himself of the protection of that country.

Under the Immigration and Asylum Act 1999 the government has an obligation to provide financial support to asylum seekers who are destitute. The National Asylum Support Service provides asylum seekers with vouchers for food and any other goods they feel they need and £10 cash per week. Accommodation is also provided on a 'no choice' basis.

As the government has made clear:

The United Kingdom has a proud tradition of providing a safe haven for genuine refugees. The UK Government is determined to ensure that genuine refugees are properly protected and that there is no incentive for people who wish to migrate for other reasons to misuse asylum procedures . . . Those who are recognised as refugees will be granted immediate settlement in the UK and will be helped to build a new life.

(Source: www.ind.homeoffice.gov.uk/default.asp?pageid=15)

Questions

1 'Something needs to be done about the young generation as they are out of control.' Do you accept or reject this statement? Write one paragraph to support your view.

2 Prime Minister Tony Blair recently suggested a plan to withhold child benefits from the parents of 'young tearaways'. Do you agree with such a policy? State at least three reasons for your answer.

3 What would you include in a programme of citizenship education for 16 to 19-year-olds?

4 Outline the arguments for and against the introduction of a citizenship strand into the National Curriculum.

5 In 2000, while David Blunkett was Home Secretary, he suggested that before immigrants could be given British citizenship they should have to pass a written English test and be prepared to swear an oath of allegiance to the Queen and promise to uphold British rights, values and freedoms. Do you accept or reject David Blunkett's view? Give reasons for your answer.

4

Education

Since 1945 education policy in the UK has been based upon an attempt to achieve two objectives:

- greater social justice; and
- servicing the needs of the economy.

In this chapter we shall look at how successful government policy has been in these two areas.

The Education Act 1944 established the principle for secondary education for all, *free at the point of issue,* which meant that parents did not have to pay for the education of their children – the cost was paid by local taxes. The 1944 Act also gave local authorities responsibility for looking after the physical needs of children in schools. Local education authorities (LEAs) were expected to provide free school milk or other appropriate refreshments, a school medical service, a school dental service and a school psychiatric service.

It was commonly assumed that, before the Education Act 1944, many people acquired positions of power and influence and well-paid jobs, for example in the professions, because of their social background rather than on the basis of their own individual effort and achievement. For the post-war governments social justice has meant equality of opportunity.

However, what is *equality of opportunity?* There are two very different interpretations of the term; it can mean either:

- everybody is provided with the same opportunity, but only some people will take the opportunity, which will generate an unequal society; but one might want to argue this would be inequality with a sense of fairness. People would get out what they put in; people would get what they deserve; or

key term

social justice

In terms of education policy this is associated with the attempt to achieve a *meritocracy* by having greater equality of opportunity within the education system. Michael Young first used the term 'meritocracy' in an essay published in 1957. Young argued that the ranking of social classes should be based upon the principle that people who are the hardest working and the most intelligent should be allowed to rise to the top of the class system and be given the greatest rewards. He used the formula: I + E = M, intelligence plus effort equals merit. The role of the education system was to identify the hard-working and intelligent people so that such people could be placed in the most demanding occupations.

- alternatively, equality of opportunity can also mean 'equality of outcome', in which people are given different amounts of resource, because they come into the education system with different needs and problems, with the aim of making sure that people leave the education system with the same qualifications.

You might want to reflect for a moment on which notion you agree with and list your reasons why.

It was commonly assumed that before the 1944 Act there was a pool of ability within the population that was being wasted because parents could not afford to send their children to secondary school. Following the 1944 Act LEAs were encouraged to introduce the tripartite system of education. This involved all children taking a test at the age of 11 to determine their *aptitude and ability*. The examination became known as the 11+. On the basis of the results, children were allocated to one of three different types of school:

- the grammar school – for children who enjoyed *learning for learning's sake;*
- the modern school – for children who *could deal more easily with concrete objects rather than abstract ideas;*
- the technical school – for children who had an aptitude for working in local industry.

The schools were meant to have *parity of esteem*, which meant that although the schools provided a different educational experience for the children who attended them, they were the same in terms of their status. Parents had a very different view; it was commonly assumed that if children were selected to go to the grammar school then they had *passed* the 11+.

Although the aim of the policy was to ensure that all children irrespective of class background had an equal opportunity, in the 1950s and 1960s educational achievement was still closely related to social class. Children whose parents had a professional or managerial occupation were 10 times more likely to attend university than children whose parents had unskilled manual occupations. The research at the time suggested a number of possible causes for working-class underachievement.

J.W.B. Douglas carried out a survey of all the children born in Britain during the first week in March 1946, and interviewed them periodically over their school careers. Douglas found that one major factor in the success of middle-class children was that their parents could give them effective advice and encouragement because the parents had had experience of doing well at school themselves.

Wedge and Prosser did a similar study of all the children born in the first week of March 1958 and found that children who came from large families, from low-income families and lived in poor housing were all less likely to do well at school. In addition, one in 16 children experienced all three of these disadvantages.

Following the publication of the Plowden Report *Children and their Primary Schools* in 1967, the *cultural deprivation* of working-class children was seen as a factor in educational failure. Many children came to school with hostile attitudes about education, their language skills were poor, and the children were unwilling or unable to engage with the activities taking place in the classroom. Plowden recommended a programme of 'compensatory education' to help children overcome their inadequate home background and make up for their inadequate parents. The report recommended the establishment of inner-city 'educational priority areas' in which there should be:

- an expansion of nursery provision;
- an improvement in the teacher–pupil ratio;
- higher pay for teachers;
- priority given for new school building programmes;
- more books and equipment.

Educational priority areas were to be established in areas where there were a high number of homes in which:

- parents were unemployed, low paid or claiming benefit;
- there was a high number of 'incomplete families' – one-parent families;
- there was a high number of 'retarded children' – children with special needs;
- there was a high number of families whose first language was not English.

Again the argument was that additional resources were needed to help these children gain the skills required to become gainfully employed.

Home background also figured in the research of Basil Bernstein (1970) who argued that different language codes were a key factor in education success. Jackson and Marsden in their book *Education and the Working Class* (1969) identified a class of home and school cultures as a key factor in working-class children underachieving.

In the 1970s research into working-class underachievement in education focused on processes that were taking place within the school. In particular, that teachers' expectations of working-class children were significantly lower than the expectations that they had for middle-class children. In other words, many teachers labelled children from working-class backgrounds as underachievers. David Hargreaves (1970) in his study of a secondary modern in Manchester found that teachers often disliked teaching children from working-class backgrounds because they were seen as unpleasant to teach and were more likely to be trouble-makers. This conclusion was reinforced by a study of a Manchester grammar school by Colin Lacey.

The argument here was that teachers label children on the basis of their perceived ability, and that class background is one major factor in the formation of the teachers' judgement. However the children behave, the teachers redefine the children's behaviour and their academic performance to fit in with their preconceived expectations. Children are relatively powerless to resist the label and as a consequence rebel by behaving in a disruptive manner, which of course was the teacher's initial expectation. This type of relation between cause and effect became known as a 'self-fulfilling prophecy'.

In order to make the education system more open to children from working-class backgrounds, in 1965 the Labour government issued Circular 10/65 in which they encouraged LEAs to introduce plans for *comprehensive education.* Instead of allocating children to one of three types of school after an 11+ exam, all children in a local area would go to the same school.

It was believed that such comprehensive schools would help to break down class barriers, provide greater educational equality of opportunity and provide a better-quality education for the pupils.

From the mid 1950s until the early 1970s, there was a 'baby boom' in Britain – in other words there was a significant increase in the birth rate. At the same time, the number of places at grammar school could not expand as fast. As a consequence of this, more and more able and middle-class children were sent to secondary modern schools. Many parents objected to their children being labelled as educational failures at the age of 11 and it was this factor that brought about calls for the introduction of comprehensive education. In addition, there were question marks against the validity of the 11+ tests and the problem of what to do with children who were *late developers.*

As we moved in to the 1980s, following the publication of Michael Rutter's book *Fifteen Thousand Hours,* the school remained the focus for research on educational underachievement. However, Rutter argued that schools do make a difference. There are schools that perform better than others on a range of indicators, such as examination performance, even when the class composition of the children is the same.

Rutter measured four factors:

- school attendance;
- academic achievement in public examinations;

- behaviour in school;
- rate of delinquency outside school.

He found marked variation in 12 very similar inner London secondary schools. Success was associated with teachers who were much more likely to be:

- on time;
- well-organized, patient, encouraging;
- inspirational;
- willing to share extracurricular activities with pupils;
- reliable.

In a survey of what became known as *excellent schools* research, Hedley Beare (1989) found that *effective schools* were more likely to have:

- strong leadership – in which senior teachers carefully monitored junior teachers;
- a climate of expectation;
- an orderly atmosphere;
- an instructional focus;
- careful monitoring of students – with minimum levels of achievement.

The main thrust of the Conservative government's education policy from 1979 to 1997 was based upon the assumption that schools do make a difference. In 1980, 1981, 1986 and 1988 the government passed Education Acts that significantly enhanced the rights of parents in relation to schools.

Education Act 1980

- Parents had the right to be elected by other parents to the school's governing body.
- The right to see minutes of governors' meeting.

Education Act 1981

- Parents had the right to what they considered to be a suitable education for their child – if a child had special needs, that child could be educated in a mainstream school if the parents wished it.

Education Act 1986

- Parents had the right to an annual meeting with the governors.
- Parents had the right to see information about the financial affairs of the school.

- Parents had the right to appeal if their child was excluded from school for more than five days.

Education Act 1988

- Open enrolment, parents had the right to apply for their child to go to the school of their choice.
- The National Curriculum was introduced.
- National assessment at the ages of seven, 11, 14 and 16.
- Parents could call for a ballot to take the school out of local authority control.
- Local management of schools, school governors became responsible for the running of the school.

Schools now had to compete with each other for pupils. Moreover, pupils brought with them an amount of money from the local authority to pay for their education. The budget of the school was not allocated by a political decision of a local education authority but was formed in the market place. The more pupils that went to a school the bigger was its budget. In such a market place 'good' schools would expand and 'poor' schools would contract and eventually close unless they could raise their standards in the eyes of parents.

In order to make sure that schools were performing to an acceptable standard, and to give some additional objective data upon which parents could base their judgement on how effective schools were in providing education, in 1993 Ofsted (the Office for Standards in Education) was formed. With the formation of Ofsted every school is inspected fully every four years. Teams of inspectors are from private companies, which bid for contracts to inspect individual schools. The tenders are given to inspection teams on the basis of the value for money that they offer – the cost of the inspection – and the experience of the people in the inspection teams. After an inspection a report is published and a summary is sent to all parents of children in the school. The school has to draw up an action plan to address any weaknesses identified by the inspectors.

Michael Apple

Marxists have been highly critical of 'New Right/neoliberal' education policy in both the US and Europe, such as that introduced by the Conservative government in Britain in the 1980s.

Michael Apple begins his book *Ideology and Curriculum* (1979) with two points that are of central concern to Marxists who are interested in education:

- The role of the education system in the reproduction of labour power.

- The role of the education system in propagating and maintaining ideology.

> *Cultural institutions like schools . . . control of the knowledge preserving and producing institutions is critical in enhancing the ideological hegemony of dominant classes, since these institutions are often sites at which ideologies are produced within the common sense of students.*

Apple draws upon the work of Althusser, *Ideology and the Ideological State Apparatuses* (1971). In capitalism 'submission to the rules of the established order' must be ensured. This involves the reproduction of submission to the ruling ideology for the workers and reproduction of the ability to manipulate the ruling ideology correctly for the agents of exploitation and repression.

Apple also draws upon the work of Antonio Gramsci who argued that the state rules by consent – but can use force if necessary. The state attempts to form a *historic bloc,* which involves making compromises with different groups on an effort to maintain solidarity. Consent is maintained by *hegemony* – a body of ideas, which becomes part of our consciousness, and which we accept as right. Capitalism can be overthrown only by challenging and reformulating hegemony and establishing a new historic bloc.

For Apple, hegemony is:

> *the most helpful way of thinking through the complex characteristics, the scope and varied functions of ideology is found in the concept of hegemony. The idea that ideological saturation permeates our lived experience, enables one to see how people can employ frameworks which both assist them in organizing their world and enable them to believe they are neutral participants in the neutral instrumentation of schooling, while at the same time, these frameworks serve particular economic and ideological interests which are hidden from them.*

Apple accepts the distinction that Marx made between:

- true consciousness – where people are aware of their economic interests and their attitudes support those interests; and
- false consciousness – where people are unaware of their economic interests.

For Apple, ideologies can be looked at in a number of ways: 'They can be more or less coherent sets of social beliefs that guide our actions and serve particular social interests' and 'They are also a complex assemblage of common-sense meanings and practices embodied within our institutions.'

For Apple, schools process people. They assist in selecting and certifying a workforce for a hierarchical labour market. Moreover, schools teach 'differential social messages' by race, sex and class depending on one's probable destination in the labour market.

Apple also argues that schools *process knowledge*. 'They help to define certain groups' knowledge as legitimate, while other knowledge is considered inappropriate as school knowledge.'

Finally Apple argues that schools also play a critical role in the *production of knowledge:*

> *That is, our educational institutions are in part organised so that the technical/administrative knowledge needed for the division and control of labour, for expanding markets and stimulating needs, and for technical innovation is produced.*

Explain whether you agree or disagree with Apple's analysis.

analyse this

the hidden curriculum

One of the central concepts that Marxists draw upon in the study of education is the notion of the *hidden curriculum*. This concept is used to explain that whatever the teacher is discussing in class, underpinning the explicit message is an implicit message which is supportive of capitalism and inequality. But what do you think of the concept of a hidden curriculum? Read the passages by Apple below and answer the questions.

> *Different kinds of ideological meanings and practices work through the overt and hidden curriculum in schools. Ideologies not only of class, but of race and gender relations interact within the institution.*
>
> *Schools and culture have some degree of 'relative autonomy'. They are the sites of complex ideological struggles, not passive reflections of bourgeois values.*

However, Apple rejects the 'conspiracy theory' of schooling:

> *This process of reproduction is not caused (in the strong sense of that concept) by an elite group of managers who sat or now sit around tables plotting ways to 'do in' their workers at both the workplace and the school.*

Questions

1. In you own words explain what Marxists understand by the hidden curriculum.
2. Apple rejects the 'conspiracy theory' of schooling, but the key question then becomes, how is it possible for an ideology to emerge 'objectively' and only benefit one class?

Relativism is a key problem for Apple's analysis. For Apple:

> *There is an obvious danger . . . one that should not go unrecognised. To make the actual stuff of curriculum problematic, to hold what currently counts as legitimate knowledge up to ideological scrutiny, can lead to a rather vulgar brand of relativism.*

In his book *Cultural Politics and Education* (1996), Apple argues that the neoconservative/neoliberal push for restructuring education derives from an old and deep-seated conviction that the hierarchy of social class in existence in the US needs to be defended.

The neoconservatives/neoliberals, or 'New Right' argue that class hierarchy rests upon merit, educational and otherwise, and that competitive market orientations are the decisive factors propelling society onward. In his book *Official Knowledge: Democratic Education in a Conservative Age* (1999), Apple argued:

> *A particular concern will be how ideologies actually become a part of the popular consciousness of class and class fractions who are not among the elite. In order to understand this, I shall employ theoretical work on the nature of how ideology functions.*

analyse this

alternatives to school

It could be argued that school has little to do with *education* but a lot to do with control of the population.

Ivan Illich, in his 1970 work *Deschooling Society,* is critical of the *liberal* approach to education. John Dewey (1953) had argued that education was to encourage individuals to develop their full potential – their intellectual, physical, emotional and spiritual talents, and that formal education was vital for democracy. Illich, by contrast, makes the following remarks:

> *Rich and poor alike depend on schools and hospitals which guide their lives, form their world view, and define for them what is legitimate and what is not. Both view doctoring oneself as irresponsible, learning on one's own as unreliable.*
>
> *For both groups the reliance on institutional treatment renders independent accomplishment suspect.*
>
> *The poor have always been socially powerless. The increasing reliance on institutional care adds a new dimension to their helplessness: psychological impotence, the inability to fend for themselves.*

[T]he majority is already hooked on school . . . they are schooled in a sense of inferiority towards the better schooled.

[T]he existence of school discourages and disables the poor from taking control of their own learning.

All over the world the school has an anti-educational effect on society.

A second major illusion on which the school system rests is that most learning is the result of teaching.

Most people acquire most of their knowledge outside school. School has become a 'place of confinement'. Deschooling education involves: 'separating learning from social control'.

- Pupils have little or no control over what they learn or how they learn it.
- Students may have thought that the purpose of education was to provide them with skills, knowledge and qualifications, but the hidden curriculum taught them how to work and obey.
- The right to make decisions is handed over to professionals, undermining the power of ordinary people to make their own decisions.
- Students are instructed by an authoritarian teaching regime and to be successful, must conform to its rules.
- Schools prepare students for their role as mindless consumers, to whom the passive consumption of the goods and services is an end in itself.
- Schools are the most vital stage in the creation of the mindless, conforming and easily manipulated citizen.

In place of schools, Illich proposes:

- skill exchanges in which instructors teach to others the skills they use in everyday life, by the use of 'drills' (systematic instruction);
- learning webs – individuals who meet on their own initiative to discuss an issue of common concern.

One critique of Illich's position is from Bowles and Gintis who argued, in 1976, that schools are not the basis of the problem – capitalism is the basis of the problem.

Question

Look at the summary of Ivan Illich's 1970 work, *Deschooling Society* above. Do you agree with Illich or not? Give reasons for your answer.

Questions

1. Is success in the education system based solely upon individual effort and achievement or is educational success based upon the type of school that you attend, or are factors such as your social class background more significant?

2. What do you understand by the term *equality of opportunity*?

3. In the sections above we have outlined a number of possible explanations for limited scholastic achievement:

   - The *cultural deprivation* explanation in which working-class children lack such things as supportive parents, language skills and a positive attitude towards learning in schools.
   - The *material disadvantage* explanation that suggests that working-class children lack material things such as warm rooms to do their homework.
   - The *teacher expectations* explanation, in which teachers label working-class children as underachievers.
   - The *effective schools* explanation, which suggests that some schools are better than others at giving children a 'good' education.

   Which explanation do you find the most convincing? Give reasons for your answer.

4. Do you accept or reject Ivan Illich's view that we should disestablish school? State the reason for your answer.

5

Do we live in an information society?

Global governance, international organizations and Islamophobia

According to Manuel Castells, the end of the twentieth century saw the emergence of a new global economy. This global economy was a new form of capitalism characterized by three essential features:

- The core economic activities are global – strategically crucial economic activities, from capital markets to specialized labour, management and entertainment, are global in nature.
- Productivity and competitiveness were a function of knowledge generation and information processing – these network-oriented communication and information technologies provided the infrastructure for the global economy.
- Firms and territories were organized in networks of production – the financial aspect is one of the key features of the network economy.

As Castells explains, the financial dimension of the network economy 'has the ability to extend or retrench its geometry without excessive disruption, simply by reconforming the networks of investment and trade. This occurs in instants, in an endless flow of circulation.'

Over the course of the twentieth century Britain became increasingly involved in a range of international organizations, in areas as diverse as trade, security, nuclear power and biodiversity. Involvement in international organizations is based upon the assumption that countries working together can achieve more than they could alone. However, there is a price to pay. International organizations can only function efficiently if each member state gives up part of its sovereignty. In other words, international organizations can only function efficiently if each member state gives up a part its ability to act freely. In this section we shall look at:

- the information society;
- global governance;
- sovereignty;
- the Commonwealth, United Nations, European Union, NATO;
- the Aid relationship;
- September 11 and Islamophobia.

What is the 'information society'?

Castells argues that the concept of the 'information society' (*johoka shakai*) is a Japanese invention. This information society not only makes use of information technology – its social structure is shaped by the informational paradigm. It is a network society, characterized by increasing globalization.

In 1982 Ankie Hoogvelt described the political/economic arrangements within the world system in the following way:

> *the global distribution of wealth and poverty is seen as a result of market forces reinforcing an accident of history which gave a head start to the European nations. But there is also political interference in the market. While the single world market rewards some activities and penalises others, the actors can and do interfere with the operation of the world market by appealing to their nation-states to interfere on their behalf. And once we get a difference in strength of the state machinerie's, we get the operation of unequal exchange imposed by strong states on weak ones in peripheral areas – by core areas on peripheral areas. In this way capitalism involves not only appropriation of the surplus value by an owner from a labourer but an appropriation of the whole world economy by core areas.*

There has been speculation that an information society would contain:

- changes in the nature of the workforce;
- increased awareness of the value of information as a resource;
- appreciation of the need for widespread computer literacy;
- wholesale diffusion of information technologies;

key terms

globalization

In the 1990s the notion of globalization became a central concept across all of the social sciences. What underpinned the notion of globalization was the idea that the world was becoming a single place in that barriers of an economic, cultural and political nature were breaking down. Arjun Appadurai (1989) explains that the notion of political/cultural globalization is brought about by a number of flows:

- ethnoscapes – the flow of people, tourists, immigrants, refugees, exiles and guest workers;
- technoscapes – the movement of technology;
- finanscapes – the rapid movement of money via money markets and stock exchanges;
- mediascapes – information and images generated and distributed by film, television, newspapers and magazines; ▶

- ideoscapes – the movement of political ideas and ideologies.

It is commonly assumed that:

- globalization is irreversible and inevitable;
- globalization will provide the rich minority with an improved quality of life;
- globalization can make people more active and competent;
- education and training can save people from impoverishment.

However, you might want to cast doubt upon these assumptions.

deregulation and privatization

The argument here is that more economic liberalization and greater deregulation of markets will always increase the efficiency of companies and the total output of the world economy. More-over, any attempt to reverse global processes would be almost impossible and highly unfavourable.

- government intervention in support of the key enabling technologies of computing, microelectronics and telecommunications.

In 1990 Naisbitt and Aburdene argued that, in the economic sphere, there has been a shift from industrial production to service provision and as a consequence the occupational structure has changed. The 'service class' has become much more significant in the stratification system. Technology has become mainly concerned with processing information rather than processing raw materials. Self-sustaining economic growth becomes central to the process of social change. The lifelong acquisition of knowledge becomes one of the central elements of the value system of the information society.

Yoneji Masuda (1980) also presents a very optimistic vision of the information society, which he describes as a form of society 'with highly intellectual creativity where people may draw future designs on invisible canvas and pursue and realize individual lives worth living.'

In this society *information* is to become the axis of socio-economic development:

- Self-production of information will increase.
- We see the emergence of a *synergetic economy* in which, according to Masuda, 'each person cooperates and acts from his or her own standpoint in solving common problems'.
- Politically the information society is a participatory democracy, which places an emphasis upon 'the realisation of time value' (Masuda, 1980, p.33) a form of society in which all people can enjoy a worthwhile life.
- Morally, the information society is built upon a spirit of globalism and living ethically with each other and nature.

Bell 'the coming of post-industrial society'

In 1973 Daniel Bell argued that we were moving beyond the industrial model of society, for Bell we were on the brink of an 'information society' characterized by:

- A shift from manufacturing to services.
- Centrality of new science-based industries.
- The rise of a new technological elite and transformed forms of stratification.

In Bell's information society 'theoretical knowledge' became the key source of value as information technology became applied to all aspect of society.

The central theme running through the book is that scientific and technological change has resulted in 'ideology' becoming replaced by 'technical decision making' in society.

There has been a change in the character of knowledge, more theoretical knowledge, more 'codification of knowledge into abstract systems'.

There are five dimensions to Bell's post-industrial society:

- Occupational distribution: the pre-eminence of the professional and technical class.
- Economic sector: the change from a goods producing to a service economy.
- Axial principle: the centrality of theoretical knowledge as the source of innovation and of policy formulation for the society.
- Future orientation: the control of technology and technological assessment.
- Decision making: the creation of a new 'intellectual technology'.

Bell argues that decision making has become much less emotional and expressive and much more calculating and instrumental in nature. The impact of this shift can be seen in social relations, power structures and culture. The changes that Bell identifies have a significant impact of class and class analysis.

In contrast to Marx, who argued that the working class was the key group in bringing about in social change, the major class within the post-industrial society is a professional class, who have knowledge rather than property. Bell explains that this professional class is made up of four *estates:*

- the scientific;
- the technological;
- the administrative;
- the cultural.

Bell outlined what he considered to be the significance of post-industrial society:

- It strengthens the role of science and cognitive values as a basic institutional necessity of the society.
- By making decisions more technical, it brings the scientist or economist more directly into the political process.
- By deepening existing tendencies toward the bureaucratization of

intellectual work, it changes the traditional definitions of intellectual pursuits and values.

- By creating and extending a technical intelligentsia, it raises crucial questions about the relation of the technical to the literary intellectual.

Giddens' critique of Bell

- First, Giddens (1989) questions the assumption that information is becoming the main basis of the economic system and that this has resulted in a shift from manufacturing occupations to service occupations.
- Giddens argues that a majority of workers have always worked outside of manufacturing, either in agriculture or services.
- The important change in the occupation structure has been the shift from agriculture to other types of employment.
- Giddens argues that Bell assumes that the service-sector is a heterogeneous group in the population.
- In Giddens view, many service sector employees have manual occupations, for example petrol pump attendants.
- In addition, many white-collar workers are experiencing 'deskilling', which causes damage to their market and work situation and places them in a position similar to many people in manufacturing occupations.
- Bell uses the US as his model of the post-industrial society; however, the US has many specific characteristics that make it unsuitable as a typical model.

Giddens listed a number of differences in an earlier book: the size of the USA, its largely immigrant population, greater possibilities for upward social mobility, the absence of a feudal past, rich material resources and a large underclass.

Manuel Castells: the network society

Castells argues that there needs to be a full reassessment of the key assumptions and arguments of Bell and other post-industrial society theorists. In the informational paradigm the uses of technology cannot be separated from technology itself. Science and scientific activity, with the possible exception of the development of some military hardware, is conducted within a shared logic of uncensored networks of interaction and feedback, largely outside of the control of national governments

In the information society women have entered the informational workforce and undermined the structure of the traditional patriarchal family.

Castells argues that a number of taken-for-granted elements of traditional patriarchal families have been questioned:

- interpersonal relationships between the two members of the couple;
- the professional life of each member of the household;
- the economic association of the members of the household;
- the distribution of domestic work;
- the raising of the children;
- sexuality.

New forms of socialization are taking individuals out of the traditional pattern of the patriarchal family and into role redefinition, interpersonal relationships and diverse family roles which are an expression of self.

For Castells the whole world becomes interconnected in its economic functions through selective information and communications flows:

> *the purposeful, repetitive, programmable sequences of exchange and interaction between physically disjointed positions held by social actors in organisations and institutions of society.*

The networks of flows are unstable and constantly change. They generally work within the social structure at several levels:

- Networks shape the distinctions in terms of power, wealth and prestige within societies.
- Networks organize the positions of actors, organizations and institutions in societies and the position of the society within the global economy.
- Networks have a structural hierarchy, and position within is related to amount of influence an individual or institution can have on the direction of the flow within the network:

> *The structural domination of the organizational logic of the networks and of the relational logic of flows has substantial consequences that are often considered as indicators of the new informational society. In fact, they are the manifestation of a deeper trend: the emergence of flows as the stuff from which our societies are made.*

Global governance: an outline of some key institutions

'Investing' or 'pooling' sovereignty

In an effort to resolve global problems, states 'invest' or 'pool' sovereignty in international organizations, as the following extract from Horsman and Marshall (1994) makes clear:

The increases in the number of intergovernmental organizations has been phenomenal. In 1909, there were 37; by 1951, after the post-war reconstruction, there were 123; by 1984, the number had reached 365. The constituency of these organizations varied widely: the UN, with universal scope encompassing many agencies of its own; regional bodies, such as the European Community or the Organization of African States; and a host of sectoral bodies and others with limited agendas and mandates . . . With these organizations came another slow change, but one which its advocates thought could have a more profound effect: an attempt to introduce rules into international relations, in the form of a profusion of treaties and agreements between states . . . around six thousand bilateral treaties came into force in the period 1946–55; ten thousand between 1955 and 1965; and fourteen thousand in the decade that followed. In the first decade international organizations were party to some six hundred treaties; in the second over a thousand; and in the third, over two thousand. Most of these concerned economic subjects – co-operation, trade, aid and communications. Some, such as the United Nations Declaration on Human Rights, and the agreements of the Council of Europe, were devoted to incorporating an element of morality in international relations. The result was a gradual enmeshing of states in treaties, organizations and regular meetings.

© 1994, Horsman and Marshall

The Commonwealth

The 2001 Report of the Commonwealth Secretary-General posed the following question:

Which other association enables the Heads of Government of Barbados, Lesotho or Tuvalu to sit down at a table as sovereign equals and share their concerns with the leaders of Canada, India, South Africa or the United Kingdom?

The Commonwealth is a voluntary association of 54 diverse independent sovereign countries with a common heritage and a shared commitment to a number of core values: democracy, good governance, human dignity and equality. As the Heads of Government made clear in the Coolum Declaration of 5 March 2002:

We stand united in . . . our determination to work to eliminate poverty, to promote people-centred and sustainable development, and thus progressively to remove the wide disparities in living standards among us.

The Declaration of Commonwealth Principles, 1971

In 1971 the heads of countries outlined a set of principles that stated that they believe in:

- the liberty of the individual;

- equal rights for all citizens regardless of race, colour, creed or political belief;
- the inalienable right of individuals to participate by means of free and democratic political processes in framing the society in which they live;
- racial prejudice as a dangerous sickness threatening the healthy development of the human race;
- racial discrimination as an unmitigated evil of society;
- opposition to all forms of colonial domination and racial oppression;
- commitment to the principles of human dignity and equality;
- the wide disparities in wealth now existing between different sections of mankind are too great to be tolerated;
- freest possible flow of international trade on terms fair and equitable to all;
- international co-operation is essential to remove the causes of war, promote tolerance, combat injustice and secure development among the peoples of the world.

Many people are convinced that the Commonwealth is one of the most fruitful associations for these purposes.

These principles were reaffirmed in 1991 at the Heads of Government meeting in Zimbabwe. Moreover, the Harare Commonwealth Declaration also stated that members states intended to focus and improve Commonwealth co-operation in these areas.

The Commonwealth's governance and structures

The Commonwealth today is made up of a mixture of inter-governmental, semi-governmental or non-governmental organizations. However, the key decisions are made by the Heads of Government meetings.

Commonwealth Secretariat

The day-to-day running of the Commonwealth is in the hands of the Commonwealth Secretariat, which is overseen by:

- Steering Committee of Senior Officials (SCOSO);
- finance committee;
- Board of Representatives (BOR);
- Commonwealth Fund for Technical Co-operation (CFTC).

However, at the Heads of Government meeting in 2002 it was suggested that these four bodies should be replaced by one Board of Governors, on which all Commonwealth governments would be represented and chaired by a senior official of a member country, who would be elected by the Board. It was also suggested that the Board of Governors should meet annually (in May) to give strategic direction on major policy issues, review implementation of Heads of Governments' decisions, and approve strategic plans and budgets.

For a full account of the Commonwealth's governance and structures you should look at the following website: www.chogm2002.org/pub/statements/hlrg.html.

analyse this

the value of membership of the Commonwealth

The Commonwealth is generally defined as a voluntary association of independent sovereign states consulting and co-operating in the common interests of their peoples and in the promotion of international understanding and world peace. For most members this means that the Commonwealth is less important than the UN or regional economic organizations. It has regular meetings of heads of states, but it is not a strong association of committed stakeholders such as the EU. However, the Commonwealth has valuable strengths.

- The Commonwealth's informality and voluntary nature implies that it can apply and expand its rules with remarkable ease. It has been effective on issues of decolonization and the dismantling of the apartheid system. Withdrawal or suspension of membership has also been used as a sanction.
- Members negotiate with each other without threat of force. This flexibility and the non-treaty basis of the association allow for continual growth and evolution without elaborate and extended treaty processes and a costly bureaucracy.
- English is the common language and this provides a major advantage for communication.
- Practically all members share a common heritage, traditions and constitutional history. This implies that over the entire spectrum of human endeavour the rules of governance, practice and procedures of institutions in Commonwealth countries are to some extent similar.
- The Commonwealth is a cross-section of the globe.
- It has achieved advanced standards in some areas.
- Finally, the Commonwealth is an association of peoples as well as governments. It constitutes a unique network of networks.

The following qualities of the Commonwealth also need to be mentioned:

- It has a shared vision – although member states' approach to governance varies widely, the consensus expressed on the key political, developmental and economic values gives the Commonwealth the strength of unified purpose in influencing policy both among its membership and in wider international forums.
- Flat organization – in contrast to the hierarchical, command and control models favoured for much of the twentieth century, the overall absence of administrative tiers between its autonomous heads of state/government and the Secretariat give the Commonwealth the flexibility to respond quickly and imaginatively to new demands and complex issues.
- Distributed network – in a similar way, the Commonwealth's networked organization, in which power, creativity and resources are widely dispersed but easily and rapidly focused on new challenges and targets, is now the common goal of the large companies world wide.
- Rich knowledge assets – as a relative value of knowledge in the global economy and individual organizations increases, strategic effort is now being geared towards identifying and mobilizing this resource in ways long familiar to the nations and peoples of the Commonwealth.

(Source: www.chogm2002.org/pub/statements/hlrg.html)

Question

According to the passage, what are the benefits for a country joining the Commonwealth? Make a list of the reasons you agree with and a list of reasons you disagree with, stating the reasons for your answer.

analyse this

Below are a number of international agreements that the British government has signed up to. Search newspaper databases and the internet and write a short paragraph outlining the commitment that the UK government has made in each case.

- OECD Harmful Tax Initiative;
- The Fancourt Declaration;
- UN Millennium Declaration;
- the Millennium Development Goals – the Financing for Development Conference (Monterrey, Mexico, 18–22 March 2002);
- The World Summit on Sustainable Development (Johannesburg, August/September 2002 – groundbreaking proposal from Africa to tackle poverty through the New Partnership for Africa's Development).

The United Nations (UN)

The United Nations was formed after the Second World War and had its first general assembly meeting in London on 10 January 1946. The UN, like the League of Nations that preceded it, attempts to provide a forum for:

- the quiet resolution of quarrels on the lines of trust, impartiality, universal justice and international law;
- the open hearing of pleas from all participants in a quarrel in front of the world's forum of justice;
- examination of the meaningful facts of a dispute by fair scrutiny;
- collective security – bringing the united support, including military support, of all its members to work opposing armed assault;
- encouraging international economic and social cooperation.

In terms of its constitution, power is given to the Security Council, which has five permanent members: the US, Russia, China, France and Britain together with six non-permanent members elected by the General Assembly for a two-year period, with half retiring each year. Each of the members of the Security Council has a veto over the decisions of the Security Council. What is significant about the Security Council is that its decisions are binding upon all members of the United Nations, hence the non-Security Council members have surrendered their sovereignty to the United Nations, yet the veto means that the members of the Security Council have their sovereignty left intact.

Moreover, the UN does not confine its powers to its own members, but will take steps to prevent aggression from non-member states.

The other important body within the UN is the General Assembly. This gives all members of the UN an opportunity to discuss issues that are of concern however, its decisions are not binding upon the Security Council but are treated as 'recommendations'. The UN also has a Secretariat, which is under the control of the Secretary General, who can bring any issue to the attention of the Security Council that the Secretary General believes can endanger the continuance of world peace.

Article 100 of the UN charter attempts to put beyond doubt the independence of the Secretary General and the Secretariat. It states that: 'In the performance of their duties, the Secretary General and the staff shall not seek or receive instructions from any government or from any authority external to the Organisation. They shall refrain from any action that might reflect on their position as international officials accountable only to the Organisation.'

The UN also has a number of agencies such as the World Health Organization (WHO), and the United Nations Educational, Scientific and

Cultural Organization (UNESCO). There is also the International Court of Justice, which is made up of 15 judges. All member states agree to comply with its decisions. However, member states do not have to state in advance if they will accept as binding any decision of the UN that might affect them. The significance of these agencies and the court is that they provide the population of the world with a clear idea of the citizenship rights. In areas such as health, education and justice, all members of the human race can expect the UN minimum from their national governments. In this sense the activities of the UN agencies and the court can be viewed as a form of cultural globalization.

The UN was established to prevent international conflict, but many nations in the post-war period still placed their trust in alliances that held a balance of power. Many nations felt unable to place their security needs into the hands of the UN. The North Atlantic Treaty Organization (NATO) is an example of an organization that has, for most of the post-war period, attempted to hold the balance of power in the world. One possible consequence of balance of power alliances, a trivial dispute escalating into a major conflict, was clearly outlined by Crowley (1963):

> *One of the reasons for the emergence of the League of Nations after 1918 was the fact that First World War provided a notable instance of this. Germany was allied with Austria, Russia with France; Russia regarded herself as the protector of Serbia, and Britain had an understanding with France. A single act of murder, the victim being the heir to the Austrian Imperial throne, resulted in Austria presenting an ultimatum to Serbia; Russia came to Serbia's assistance; Germany and France were drawn in almost immediately. So also, within a few days, was Britain, and eventually most of the world was involved. The result was the horror of 1914–18.*

In terms of issues of national sovereignty, what is significant about NATO is that member states – USA, Britain, Canada, Holland, Belgium, Luxembourg, Denmark, Norway, Iceland, Italy, Greece, Germany, Turkey, Portugal and France (although France is part of NATO's political structure but not its military command structure) – have given control of their defence force to an international organization. The purpose of NATO was to defend Europe and North America against the former Soviet Union and its allies, which themselves had a military alliance formed in 1955 under the Warsaw Treaty.

The European Union

The European Union (EU) is also a major institution involved in the dissolution of the nation state and its loss of sovereignty. The EU has its origins in three institutions: the European Economic Community (EEC) – a free trade area also known as the Common Market; Euratom, a body created to coordinate joint development of nuclear power; and the European Coal and Steel Community, established to increase the efficiency of these industries by facilitating greater competition. With the Maastricht

Treaty, the EU became a political union moving towards full economic and monetary union with a central bank, a common currency, and a common social policy, including a 'social chapter' that gives all EU citizens a minimum wage and common employment rights. Many people in Britain fear that we may be losing are national identity because of greater European integration.

World trade is another area in which there are international bodies that diminish the sovereignty of national governments. In 1947, 35 countries signed up for the General Agreement on Tariffs and Trade (GATT), in which all members agreed not to increase tax, duties or impose restrictions on each other's goods. In 1986 GATT held a meeting in Uruguay with the intention of making significant changes to the GATT agreement. This 'Uruguay Round' dragged on into the 1990s. In the end a new organization was formed – the World Trade Organization. This has two aims: firstly, to continue the GATT agreements on opening up world trade to competition; and secondly, to make world trade more responsible for the environment. On 24 March 1995 Renato Ruggiero became head of the WTO. He was reported by *The Times* as saying: 'We cannot go back to the protectionism of the 1930s. Trade is the main tool of globalisation.' He was also reported as saying that the world had a vested interest in bringing both China and Russia fully into the world system: 'They must respect the rules of the game. But we have to adapt all international institutions to globalisation.'

The aid relationship

One of the major global issues in the 1980s and 1990s was that of aid. This issue shows more clearly than any other the argument between sociologists over global issues. As Best (2000, 2002) makes clear, aid is the giving of resources from one country to another and it can take a number of different forms:

- Development aid – this is given to help a country develop its economy or services in an effort to improve the quality of life for all people in the country.
- Emergency aid – this is given after a disaster, such as famine or flood.
- Military aid – this can include expertise as well as weapons.
- Project aid – this is aid given for specific projects such as a dam, a school or a road. It is often referred to as 'tied' aid because the donor country usually has some control over the project, such as insisting that purchases made with the aid come from the donor country.
- Programme aid – this is aid which is not linked to specific projects, it could be used to improve a country's trade imbalance.

Aid can be either bilateral, when one country gives help to another, or multilateral, in which countries give money to a international body such as the World Bank.

However, according to Teresa Hayter, western governments use the aid relationship to support pro-capitalist governments in the world:

> *The World Bank and the IMF . . . are dominated by the major Western powers; the United States and half a dozen other governments have an effective veto over their lending decisions through the weighted voting system, and other more subtle ways. In addition, the World Bank raises around 80 per cent of its money through Wall Street and other private financial markets; this means that they must defend the interests of those markets..*

Hayter's view is that the World Bank and the IMF will only provide aid or loans if the country is prepared to manage its economy in a way that the Bank or the IMF approve of. The World Bank and the IMF insist upon 'structural adjustments' or 'stabilization programmes'. Hayter explains the nature of such programmes:

> *The stabilisation, or structural adjustment, programmes have been programmes to control government spending and the balance of payments by orthodox liberal means: by limiting credit, cutting public social expenditure and sometimes public investment, keeping down or cutting wages, eliminating subsidies, and devaluation. Cuts in military expenditure are not demanded; the issue is said to be 'too sensitive'. For example the government of Morocco, with the approval of the World Bank and the IMF, has been carrying out a programme of cuts in domestic public expenditure, especially on food subsidies which benefit the poor; at the same time it has been spending large sums on the war in the Sahara.*

However, possibly the most astonishing truth about the aid relationship is that most aid goes to states that are economically well off. In 1992 the British government, for example, gave more aid to the oil-rich state of Oman than it did to poverty-stricken Ethiopia. Moreover, many aid-funded development schemes have 'strings attached'. A notorious British example was the Pergau dam project in Malaysia, built by Balfour Beatty and Cementation. The dam cost £397 million to construct, of which Britain gave £234 million in aid. However, it was suggested that the aid was directly linked to arms deals worth £1.3 billion to British companies.

September 11

Since the terrorist attacks in the US on 11 September 2001 the international 'war on terrorism' has been the main focus of international cooperation.

Was there a religious motive behind the September 11 attacks? In 1998 Osama bin Laden, the leader of the terrorist group al-Qaeda, declared a *jihad* against the US: 'To kill Americans and their allies, both civil and military, is an individual duty of every Muslim who is able, in any country . . . until their armies, shattered and broken-winged, depart from all the lands of Islam.' Bin Laden believes that violence, including killing civilians, is justified as a means to restore *sharia* (Islamic law) and maintain Islamic cultural identity. However, although bin Laden often quotes the Koran and promotes a fundamentalist interpretation of Islam, bin Laden is not a certified Islamic cleric and most Muslims do not accept his fundamentalist, radical and politicized interpretation of Islam. In addition, few Muslims support these extreme views. The September 11 attacks were widely condemned across the Muslim world.

Islamophobia

Following the collapse of communism, Francis Fukuyama in *The End of History and the Last Man* (1992) argues that history, in terms of new great historical epochs (such as socialism, communism, fascism), has come to an end and from this moment on we shall have 'events' that take place within a form of liberal capitalism that we all share. Fukuyama suggests that cultural globalization is bringing about a homogenization of all civilization upon one liberal democratic model. For Fukuyama, liberal democracy is the end point or terminus of history.

However, a contrasting and very pessimistic view has been suggested by Samuel Huntington. In *The Clash of Civilizations?* Huntington argues that the confrontation of the Cold War between the US and the Soviet Union has been replaced by multiple confrontations, primarily between western democracy and Islam. These clashes are not based on politics, economics or the demands of the nation state, but rather on culture. The next world war, if there is one, he argues will be between these contrasting civilizations.

These divisions have great depth, they are old and embody basic differences between peoples. Moreover, claims Huntingdon, these conflicts will become more passionate as people struggle to keep hold of their cultural identity against the globalizing tendencies of the modern world which are seen to be western in origin.

In contrast to Huntington's view, Al-Azmeh has argued that: 'there are as many Islams as there are situations that sustain it.'

Jihad versus McWorld: a clash of cultures?

Benjamin Barber (1996) argued that in the future we are likely to see major conflicts between western commerce and consumerism (McWorld) and more localized nationalistic and religious conflicts (Jihad). The notion of McWorld is derived from George Ritzer's conception of the process of McDonaldization – the production-line approach that has been common in a number of industries for many years in the hospitality industries. Ritzer views this process as a bad thing because it is seen as reducing both diversity and choice. McDonaldization has four key components:

- Efficiency, which involves 'choosing the optimum means to a given end'. This efficiency is defined by the organization rather than the individual and is in effect imposed upon the individual.
- Calculability, in which there is 'an emphasis on the quantitative aspect of products sold (portion size, cost) and service offered (the time it takes to get the product)'.
- Predictability, in which there is 'discipline, order, systemization, formalization, routine, consistency and methodical operation. In such a society, people prefer to know what to expect in most settings and at most times.' The experience is the same in every shop for the consumer and work becomes very routine for the workers.
- Control. Management has a need to control both the workers and the customers in an effort to reduce the level of uncertainty within the organization.

However, Ritzer is critical of these processes, which he argues have their own irrational outcomes: 'Rational systems inevitably spawn a series of irrationalities that limit, eventually compromise, and perhaps even undermine their rationality.' The inefficiencies generated by these rational processes include:

- longer waiting times and more work for the customer – having to make your own salad in the salad bar, or fill up your own drink in the fast-food restaurant;
- dehumanization of the worker and of the customer;
- the emergence of unforeseen anomalies – things that go wrong without being planned for.

In contrast to Huntingdon, Barber does not see jihad as a throwback to pre-modern times – rather, it is a reaction to the western processes of McDonaldization:

> *Jihad stands not so much in stark opposition as in subtle counterpoint to McWorld and is itself a dialectical response to modernity whose features both reflect and reinforce the modern world's virtues and vices – Jihad via McWorld rather than Jihad versus McWorld. The forces of Jihad are not only remembered and retrieved by the enemies of McWorld but imagined and contrived by its friends and proponents. Jihad is not only McWorld's adversary, it is its child.*

Before we can evaluate this, we need to have a closer look at the nature of Islam.

What is Islam?

In the west there is a clear distinction between the political sphere and the religious sphere, with politics regarded in the eyes of most people as a totally secular activity. Not so with Islam. Here religion and politics are one and the same activity. The word Islam is derived from two roots: *Salm* (peace) and *Silm* (submission). Therefore, Islam stands for a commitment to surrender one's will to the will of God. For the Muslim it is through this submission to God that peace is brought about.

Islam is more than a simple faith, on the western model of religion, nor is it simply a political doctrine or ideology. It is all of these, as well as a social movement complete with an ethical code that is found in the holy book, the Qur'an, which is believed by Muslims to be the word of God, and contains the philosophical basis of a political system and the Hadiths or traditions that were passed down from the Prophet Muhammad and his companions.

Three main principles are of significance:

- *Tawhid:* the idea that there is one God who is the creator, whom we should worship alone as master of the universe. In other words, Muslims have no conception of political sovereignty outside the law of the Qur'an (*shari'a*). The purpose of government in the Islamic state is to fulfil the word of God.
- *Risala:* the medium through which Muslims receive the law of God, which provides an established model of how to lead a good Muslim way of life.
- *Khilafa:* this third element, means 'representation'. If people have any power in society they should exercise their power as the representatives of God on earth. Responsibility for the maintenance of *Khilafa* falls upon the whole Muslim community and not upon any single individual or section of society. The leader, or *amir,* should ideally be guided by an advisory council (*shura*), elected by universal sufferage, of all the people who accept the fundamentals of the constitution. In the Islamic state, all citizens have the right to be critical of the government, and the government maintains its legitimacy by seeking the active co-operation of the masses.

Underpinning the Islamic state is the principle of *La ilaha illallah* – there is no deity but God. It is from *La illaha iilallah* that the five articles of faith are derived:

- belief in one God – the *shahada;*
- the *salat* – the need to pray formally five times each day;
- the *zakat* – having concern for the poor and giving them help;

- fasting during the month of Ramadan;
- the pilgrimage to Mecca – the *hajj*.

Individuals have free will and can choose not to be Muslim. However, to choose not to be a Muslim is to become an unbeliever (a *Kafir*). The state of being *Kufr* is seen to be one of ignorance, ingratitude and infidelity. However, Islam has laid down rights for non-Muslims, referred to as *dhimmis* (the covenanted), living within the Islamic state. Moreover, these rights are an important part of the constitution. The *dhimmis* are to be respected in the same way as Muslims, with no difference in either civil or criminal law. Human rights in an Islamic society are rights conferred by God, and for a Muslim not to accept the validity of the rights of non-Muslims, or not to give non-Muslims respect, is to become one of the *Kafirun*. However, traditionally Muslims have accepted three clear forms of political inequality: between Muslims and non-Muslims; between men and women; and between masters and slaves. In more recent years Muslim social movements have expressed hostility towards equal rights for lesbian and gay people.

Many people in the west view Islamic states with mistrust and even fear, believing that the spread of Islamic fundamentalism – principally from Iran – is one of the major threats to the west. This view is reinforced by the idea of *jihad,* and the suggestion of world domination by the use of terrorism that seems to underpin this concept. The stereotyping of Islam in recent years was related to:

- The Iranian Revolution in 1979, in which the Ayatollah Khomeini and his supporters overthrew the violent and corrupt regime of the Shah and introduced a new constitution, legal code (*shari'a*), judicial system, education system and so forth, all of which were based upon Islamic principles.
- The *Satanic Verses* controversy (1989) in which Ayatollah Khomeini ordered that author Salman Rushdie should be executed for comments he had made about the Prophet Muhammad in his novel the *Satanic Verses*.
- The Gulf War (1991) in which Iraq occupied Kuwait and annexed the country as Iraq's nineteenth province.
- Attacks on the twin towers of the World Trade Center, New York on the 11 September 2001, in which two hijacked planes were flown into two large office blocks in New York, and a third into the Pentagon in Washington. A fourth crashed in Pennsylvania.

What is *jihad?*

Jihad is not one of the central pillars of Islam. However, if the citizens of an Islamic state are attacked by a non-Muslim power, then there is an obligation on all Muslims to come forward for *jihad*. In addition, it is the religious duty of the neighbouring Muslim countries to help and if they fail, then the Muslims of the whole world must fight the common enemy. The use of *jihad* is part of the defence of Islam, and is used in particular to describe a war that is waged in the name of God against people who practise oppression against Islam.

However, it is important to recognize that there is a great diversity within Islam. There are two main groups within the Muslim world: the majority Sunni who make up an estimated 90 per cent of the Muslim population and the Shi'i. The two groups split after the death of the Prophet Muhammad because of a disagreement over the status of his brother-in-law, Ali, as the only legitimate leader after the Prophet Muhammad. In addition, within these two broad groups there is much diversity. Many Shi'ites, such as the late Ayatollah Khomeini, believe that sovereignty does not lay with the people but with God. This gave many in the west the view that all Muslims were hostile to democracy.

analyse this

There is a great deal of information, argument and counter-argument regarding the events of 11 September 2001. Do an internet search and state whether, in your opinion, the war in Afghanistan was an act of revenge inflicted by an evil and corrupt state for the purpose of genocide and unimaginable suffering, or whether it was a measured attempt to bring to justice the people who attacked the World Trade Center on 11 September 2001.

6

Are the media biased?

'News' by its very nature is selective – it is what social scientists call a 'constructed reality'. News does not simply exist out there. Not everything that happens in the world can be reported, so events have to be selected as 'newsworthy' by journalists and editors. You might want to reflect for a moment on why some events are newsworthy and others are not.

Newspapers select what is newsworthy to fit in with the news values of the company that owns the newspaper. Often these news values are based on the political perspective of the newspaper. However, radio and television news have a legal obligation to be both balanced and neutral in their reporting. Since the Television Act 1954 television news has been based upon the notion of 'due impartiality', as the BBC make clear: 'Due impartiality lies at the heart of the BBC. It is a core value and no area of programming is exempt from it. All BBC programmes and services should show open-mindedness, fairness and a respect for truth.'

The BBC's charter requires the BBC to do all it can to secure that all radio and television programmes:

treat controversial subjects with due accuracy and impartiality, both in the Corporation's news services and in the more general field of programmes dealing with matters of public policy or of political or industrial controversy, and do not contain any material expressing the opinion of the Corporation on current affairs or matters of public policy other than broadcasting and matter contained in programmes in either House of Parliament or proceedings of a local authority or a committee of two or more local authorities.

(Source: www.bbc.co.uk)

key terms

balance

For most issues there are two sides or two viewpoints, and 'balance' is achieved by having a simple mathematical balance, giving equal time to each view. If the government is given two minutes of airtime, then the opposition should be given two minutes of airtime.

neutrality

Television news should refrain from 'editorializing'; in other words, broadcasters should not express an opinion that one view is superior to another view.

Due impartiality is supposed to ensure balance and neutrality. There should be a full range of views and opinions presented in news and current affairs programmes, with account taken of the weight of opinion, whilst recognizing that opinion changes. However, as Lord Annan made clear in a report into the future of broadcasting: 'The broadcasters are operating within a system of parliamentary democracy and must share its assumptions.'

Due impartiality is given to 'legitimate' political parties, but not to people who are regarded as 'terrorists'.

We could argue that 'due impartiality' assumes that the basic model of society is that of democratic consensus where a considerable measure of agreement exists over political and economic arrangements.

The term 'due' in 'due impartiality' is understood to mean adequate or appropriate to the nature of the subject and the type of programme. Two concepts underpin 'due impartiality': balance and neutrality.

However, it is important to note that 'due impartiality' is only applied to political and industrial news. In any other areas of social life, such as religious news, sports news or foreign affairs, broadcasters have no legal obligation to be either balanced or neutral.

analyse this

Consider the following example below. Do you agree or disagree with the decision of the Radio Authority to fine Virgin Radio in this case?

> *The Radio Authority announced today (16 May) that it has fined Virgin Radio £75,000 for a serious breach of the rules requiring due impartiality from broadcasters. In the Virgin Breakfast Show on 21 March 2000, Chris Evans expressed live on air, in two extended pieces, his support for Ken Livingstone in the London Mayoral Election.*

The Chair of the Authority, Richard Hooper said:

> *'Political impartiality is a cornerstone of British broadcasting, strongly supported by all governments and public opinion over many years. Radio spectrum is a scarce public resource which brings with it unambiguous obligations in the public interest. This broadcast by Virgin was a flagrant breach of the long-standing rules surrounding political impartiality, made worse by the fact that the broadcast took*

place in the run-up to that most sensitive of political events, an election. The breach also demonstrated a critical failure of compliance by the licensee, and we are determined that this shall not be repeated.

This broadcast breached section 90(3) of the Broadcasting Act 1990, which requires:

A. *where the licensed service is a national service, that due impartiality is preserved on the part of the person providing the service as respects matters of political or industrial controversy or relating to current public policy.*

B. *where the licensed service is a local, satellite and licensable sound programme service, that undue prominence is not given in its programmes to the views and opinions of particular persons or bodies on such matters.*

(Source: www.radioauthority-org/newsroom/news-release/00/pr072.html)

The Glasgow University Media Research Group

For over 25 years the Glasgow Media Group have argued that both BBC News and ITN cannot refrain from editorializing and fall short of their legal obligation to present political and industrial news in a balanced, neutral and objective fashion. From a Marxian perspective the group argues that television news:

1. Does not reflect the full range of views.
2. Is undemocratic in its choice of who is allowed to speak.
3. Broadcasters defy notions of accuracy and impartiality

Like all Marxists, the group assumes that the social structure of society is divided between two classes:

- *The bourgeoisie* – the ruling class, which owns the means of production (in other words the factories, shops and offices).
- *The proletariat* – the working class, which only owns its labour power and works for the bourgeoisie. The proletariat is exploited by the bourgeoisie because workers are not paid the true value of their labour power.

The bourgeoisie makes use of the mass media – television, newspapers, radio – to manipulate the ideas of the proletariat. The bourgeoisie do this by the effective use of ideology – a coherent set of ideas and beliefs that are imposed upon the minds of the workers. Ideology creates a false consciousness in the minds of workers, so that they are unable to see what is in their own best interests.

The group argues that the dominant ideology can be found in television news. Their first two volumes of research made a clear distinction between the distorted false consciousnesses generated by the media and the independent reality of events found in true consciousness: 'Our argument in *Bad News* Volume 1 of this study was that routine news practices led to the production of bad news. For example, viewers were given a misleading portrayal of industrial disputes in the UK when measured against the independent reality of events.'

Questions

1 Can we assume that media audiences passively accept the messages that come from television and radio? Give a reason for your answer.

2 Read the following passage. What do you think Philo and Miller are saying in the passage? Do accept or reject their arguments?

> *We define ideology as social perspectives or ways of understanding which are linked to class or other interests. In addition, our work does not simply reproduce the Marxian conception of ideology: Our studies have gone a long way beyond traditional models of the bourgeoisie and the exploited classes. We have been centrally concerned with the role of media in the mass production of misunderstanding and ignorance. We have also shown how the media do have a role in the legitimization of powerful interests and how ideologies can actually work to convince populations.*

(Source: Philo, G. and Miller, D. (2001) 'Market killing: a reply to Shaun Best', *Social Science Teacher* 31(1), p. 17

One of the key problems with the Group's research is with the manner in which they gather the data for their arguments. The group rejected conspiracy theories of the media; rather the group has always argued that news was structured and organized by taken-for-granted professional routines of journalists. Their initial research made use of content analysis in an effort to identify and measure ideology and its consequences. John Eldridge has strongly supported the use of the content analysis by the group. He argues that the content analysis is a methodologically unobtrusive measure, which can be used to analyse data without influencing what is produced. In addition, Philo and Miller also argue that content analysis can be effectively used to describe and measure ideology.

analyse this

Before we look at how the Glasgow Media Research Group made use of the content analysis, you might want to attempt one of your own.

You can do your own simple content analysis by taking two contrasting newspapers say, for example, a broadsheet such as *The Times*, the *Guardian*, or the *Independent* and a tabloid such as the *Sun*, the *Daily Mail* or the *Mirror*; or a local paper and a national paper, or paper with contrasting political views. Once you have chosen the newspapers to be contrasted, select a story that appears in both papers. For instance, if there was a story about reform of the education system, count the number of words given to the government's view and the number of words given to the opposition's view. Count the number of critical points compared to the number of positive points and count the number of emotive words used contrasted with the number of neutral words used. When you have counted these things write them down in a table. According to the people who advocate the content analysis, using such a method as the one described above will allow the true meaning of the newspapers' reports to emerge. You should be able to see by glancing at the table you have written up the bias that newspapers contain.

In more strict academic language, content analysis involves the following stages:

1. Produce a set of analytical categories in advance. In our example we chose the following analytical categories: the number of words given to the government; the number of words given to the opposition in the newspaper report of a story; the number of emotive words used; and the number of neutral words used.
2. Step two is where we apply the concepts to the text, in our case the two contrasting newspapers.
3. Step three is known as the numerical quantification. This is where we count the number of words given to the government; the number of words given to the opposition in the newspaper report of a story; the number of emotive words used and the number of neutral words used, in both of the newspapers we have selected.

The Glasgow Media Group argued:

> *Public broadcasting is committed to an ideological perspective which is founded on the view of consensus, one nation and the community. The broadcasters attempt to relay ideas which are already more or less present and interpret them for what they mistakenly see as a mass audience.*

In other words, the group found that television news was biased. News organizations had a view of the audience as a single community that shared a common view of how society should be governed and that television journalists reflected that 'one nation' view in their news reports.

However, an important methodological question here is how the group reached that conclusion from the numerical quantification of the content analysis.

Eldridge has argued: 'But we did suggest that unspoken, unacknowledged assumptions, practices or perspectives help to constitute what Goffman had called the primary framework, whereby news talk becomes meaningful.' An important methodological question here is how can the content analysis capture something such as 'unacknowledged assumptions' of journalists?

In his discussion of media institutions and journalists, Greg Philo (1995) claims: 'the routine working practices of journalists are informed by class assumptions of the society in which they live.' He adds: 'They usually wish to claim that their reportage is accurate and trustworthy, although as we show in the case studies of our original work the unconscious political assumptions which they hold produce selection and distortion which often invalidate these claims.'

Is the production of news and current affairs programmes performed in an *unconscious fashion* as Greg Philo suggests?

One of the central problems with content analysis is that, as a method of data collection, it can never tell us anything about the production of the content it describes. A criticism of the Glasgow Media Group here is that they are imposing their own opinion on television news rather than attempting an analysis of the objective data.

This means that the content analysis cannot tell us anything about the mass production of misunderstanding and ignorance. In addition, content analysis cannot tell us anything about how the audience makes sense of the news; the group assumes that we, the viewers, all view and interpret the television news in the same way.

Do you accept or reject the Group's view of passive viewer?

Ironically, in support of their arguments the group regularly makes use of what they consider to be authoritative news sources such as the *Financial Times* or *Management Today*. In other words, some sources of news should be accepted, but BBC and ITN should be rejected.

In *More Bad News* (1980) the group did give a brief defence of its use of content analysis, including the justification that content analysis can be used to make empirically valid statements about the process of news production and ideology. The group argued: 'It has been a basic contention of our approach that the detailed examination of the output of television journalism can be used to demonstrate its ideology and practices.'

How is this possible? The group's justification is: 'Since the output clearly has meaning, then the production of that meaning can as clearly be studied on the screen as it can be by interviewing either producers or audiences.'

There are a number of problems with this argument.

The group is assuming that any text – in this case a news broadcast – has only one meaning for an audience. Remember this was one of their main criticisms of television journalists – that journalists believe there is a mass audience.

Secondly the group assumes that the understanding that the audience has of the news reports is one and the same as the understanding that the group has of the report, which is clearly not the case.

Thirdly, many of the assumptions that the group makes about the process of news production, such as the key role of unconscious political assumptions, could not be studied either by content analysis or interviewing, but only implied from the data.

Fourthly, the meaning of the results produced by the content analysis depends upon which analytical categories have been used in the research. If different analytical categories are selected for use in a research project, then different results will follow.

Countering ideology

Throughout their work the group makes unjustified assumptions about the lasting nature of class and class cultures. Philo has argued that the beliefs of an individual are not a single coherent entity derived in a linear fashion from one aspect of their class position.

Greg Philo does give the reader a clear indication of how to combat the mass production of misunderstanding and ignorance. Protection from ideological distortion of the media can be achieved by:

- drawing upon one's direct experience;
- drawing upon direct contacts;
- drawing upon political culture;
- drawing upon our class experience;
- drawing upon processes of logic;
- drawing comparisons between different accounts.

On this last point Greg Philo argues that a second major reason for doubting television news arises from comparisons with other sources of information such as quality newspapers, the local press, alternative current affairs programmes and radio. As we suggested above, this raises the question of why Greg Philo holds some journalistic accounts in such high regard but holds BBC and ITN accounts in such low regard. The reasons why the group accepts as true some journalistic accounts needs some justification. Otherwise critics might argue that Greg Philo and the rest of the Group are suggesting that people who read the same quality and local press, watch the same Channel Four documentaries, share the same friends, political culture and logic as Greg Philo are liberated from ideology.

Conspiracy theory

Both the section that looked at possible bias in the media and the section on education policy had elements of *conspiracy theory* about them, but what is a conspiracy theory? And why should conspiracy theories be rejected?

Since the first broadcast of the *X-Files*, the term conspiracy theory has been commonly used to describe an outrageous, weird or even ridiculous account of why something happened in the way that it did. Such events can be political, such as conspiracy theories surrounding the assassination of President John F. Kennedy. A number of the best-known conspiracy theories are about the lives or deaths of celebrities, notably the death (or not!) of Elvis Presley, or historical events such as the moon landing in 1969, aliens from outer space (again often associated with Elvis, who was said to have been abducted by aliens).

People who put forward conspiracy theories are by and large dismissed as mistaken or mad. I recall going to hear the historian E.P. Thompson give a lecture about nuclear disarmament. When he asked for questions at the end of his presentation, someone stood up and said that one of the reasons why the vast majority of the population would not accept Thompson's views was because the government was poisoning the water supply with fluoride in order to make the population more docile and passive. Amongst the audience there was a nervous but decidedly embarrassing silence.

However, some conspiracy theorists are said to be amongst the most gifted people in society.

What is a conspiracy theory?

To *conspire* means to have a secret plan or agreement to do something that is to the detriment of others. If a conspiracy *theory* is proved to be true then it is no longer a conspiracy *theory* but a proven conspiracy. If two people *conspire* to steal a bicycle from another person – in other words, they formulate a secret plan to do something dishonest – and if the people succeed in stealing the bicycle, then they have carried out a *conspiracy*. You or I could formulate a theory to explain what happened to the bicycle:

- We could suggest that the bicycle was basically lost. (This is not a conspiracy theory.)
- We might have a sneaking suspicion that our neighbour's children hid the bicycle as a practical joke, because they've performed similar mischief in the past. This is a conspiracy theory.
- We might believe that the bicycle and its rider were abducted by aliens. This is a conspiracy theory.
- We might believe that the bicycle was taken by the police to be used in evidence against a criminal. This is not a conspiracy theory.
- We might accept a rumour, that two other people stole the bicycle. This is a conspiracy theory.

Questions

1 'Greg Philo has no concept of ideology. Ideology is merely news and views that he disagrees with.' Do you accept or reject this view of the work of the Glasgow Media Group?

2 Is content analysis an appropriate tool for doing research on ideology?

3 Are you inclined to accept or reject conspiracy theories? Give the reasons for your answer.

7

Theories of political power

Most social scientists would probably agree with Weber's view of power, which is that power is the ability to make somebody do something that you want them to do.

Max Weber made a distinction between legitimate authority and coercion. Legitimate authority is a situation in which people regard another person or group to have the right to give orders to the rest of us. In contrast, coercion is the illegitimate use of power and is often associated with the use of violence for political ends. For Weber there are three types of legitimate authority:

- *Charismatic authority.* Weber is interested here in how a political system can be upheld by the strength of a leader's character. Often charismatic leaders are believed to have almost supernatural qualities.
- *Traditional authority.* This is a political system that is upheld by continual reference to customs and traditions.
- *Rational legal authority.* This is a political system that is regarded as legitimate in the eyes of the population because it is thought to be 'legal' and built upon rational processes; the ideal type identified by Weber is the bureaucracy.

In Weber's view, modern government always results in government by bureaucracy. Hence there is a need, he claimed, for a strong parliament as a guarantor of individual rights and independence. Weber was always in favour of political democratization, and that included supporting the case in favour of votes for women. Weak parliaments generate fanatical divisions between the parties, which Weber termed 'negative politics', because it was little more than an ideological masquerade, with the important decisions taken by the state bureaucracy.

Max Weber's ideal type of bureaucracy

An ideal type is a useful model by which to measure other forms of administration. This model includes the following features:

- The organization is in the form of a hierarchy – a structure in the shape of a pyramid with a small group of people at the top with most of the power and a large group of people at the bottom with limited power.
- Bureaucratic procedures are directed by a system of theoretical or abstract rules.
- The ideal official should behave without friendship or favour to any clients.
- Bureaucrats have a rigid number of recorded duties.
- Employment in a bureaucracy is by appointment based upon qualifications, not by election.
- As a form of administration the bureaucracy has the highest degree of efficiency.

Within the bureaucracy, officials hold a set of convictions or a code of principles, which Weber termed its *Amtsehre,* and this includes:

- a recognition of the importance of their office;
- a belief in the supremacy of their own qualifications and ability;
- the opinion that the legislature or parliament is merely a talking shop;
- the belief that bureaucrats are above party politics;
- the belief that bureaucrats are the true interpreters of the national interest;
- bureaucrats have their own interests that Weber terms their *staatsrainson.*

In Weber's view, the bureaucracy is clearly defined, soulless and machine like. It is a technical mechanism for accomplishing preconceived, or pre-thought-out, objectives. However, bureaucracy has an instinctive bias to exceed its purpose, and to become an independent force within society.

The origin of bureaucratic power is knowledge, by which Weber meant the technical ability to make use of information that is protected by secrecy.

analyse this

Weber suggests that the bureaucracy is the most efficient form of administration. State whether you agree with this view. What benefits do you think a bureaucracy may have over other forms of administration? In Weber's view all bureaucratic structures make use of secrecy. What value do you think a bureaucracy can gain from secrecy?

Steven Lukes argues that Weber's conceptions of power, authority and legitimacy are too restricted in their focus. In contrast, Lukes argues that power has three dimensions, and Weber is solely concerned with the first. The three dimensions are:

- decision making, which is concerned with the actions of the decision makers;
- non-decision making, which is concerned with the way in which power is applied to restrict the scope of the decisions that the so-called decision makers can select from;
- shaping desires, which is concerned with the extent to which individuals may have their attitudes and beliefs directed by others, so as to agree to a decision that may not be in their own interests.

key terms

polyarchy

This is the most well-developed form of pluralism. According to Robert Dahl polyarchy is: 'the government of a state or city by many: contrasted with monarchy.' Poly-archy includes a set of authoritative rules assigned in response to the citizen's wishes. This is necessary for the democratic pro-cess to work. The rules guarantee our civil and political rights; which according to Lindblom (1977) include:

- freedom to form and join organizations;
- freedom of expression;

Pluralism

Pluralism describes a condition within a community in which power is widely shared amongst a multiplicity of groups and organizations, all of whom have their own sectional interests. The state is seen as the rule maker or umpire, in other words as the 'honest broker' that attempts to balance opinions within the community in an effort to strike a balance between the various sectional interests. In addition, there is always political competition and a balance between competing interests.

These rules are based upon *volitions*. Volitions are choices that are created by the citizens themselves in consultation with each other. According to Charles Lindblom, within polyarchy there is a common core of volitions:

- Simple preference: this is when a person holds a view without the need for calculated thought or reason.
- Complex judgement: this is where an individual holds a view after some consideration and analysis.
- Moral or ethical rules: this is where an individual chooses a view on the basis of a moral code.

- right to vote;
- eligibility for public office;
- right of political leaders to compete for support;
- right of political leaders to compete for votes;
- free and fair elections (open, honestly conducted, one person one vote), which will decide who is to hold the top authority;
- alternative sources of information;
- institutions for making government policies, which depend upon votes and other expressions of preference.

- Simple preference between complex judgements: this is where an individual chooses between a range of complex judgements with little calculated thought. Lindblom give the example of a person saying: 'No, I don't believe in foreign aid, but don't ask me why.'

According to Anthony Giddens all nation states have a tendency towards polyarchy. In a similar fashion, Robert Dahl argues that polyarchy is both a product of the democratizing of nation states and a type of regime. There is a high tolerance of opposition and widespread opportunities for participating in influencing the conduct of government. The institutions within polyarchy have evolved in an effort to help democratize the political process.

However, there are a number of criticisms of pluralism and polyarchy.

- Within this perspective researchers are only concerned with decision making and they ignore the idea of non-decision making.
- In addition, pluralists do not take into account that individuals may have their ideas, which we termed volitions, manipulated by others more powerful than themselves – capitalists or the mass media.
- Robert Dahl has had to accept that the unequal distribution of wealth can sustain an unequal division of political power.
- There is a problem of unrepresented or under-represented interests with the system.

All of the countries that make up the European Union together with North America, Australia and New Zealand regard themselves as pluralistic parliamentary democracies.

The Westminster Parliament

In the UK there are two Houses of Parliament: the House of Lords and the House of Commons, both of which are currently undergoing a modernization process. At present, the House of Commons is made up of 659 Members of Parliament (MPs). Each member represents a geographical area known as a *parliamentary constituency*. In England there are 529 constituencies, in Wales there are 40, in Scotland 72 and in Northern Ireland there are 18.

All the main political parties are committed to modernizing Parliament. In 1997 the House of Commons established the modernization committee, which has produced several substantive reports. In addition, the House of Commons has also debated its own modernization on a number of occasions.

Since the Great Reform Act 1832, which extended the rights of people to elect persons to the House of Commons, the House of Lords has become less important politically than the House of Commons. The Parliament Acts in 1911 and 1949 set out to reduce the influence of the House of Lords further.

More recently, people with very differing political views have expressed the concern that the House of Commons is ineffective in its scrutiny of the executive (the Prime Minister and the Cabinet) and in its scrutiny of new legislation. Eighteen years of Conservative government (1979–97), followed by a Labour government holding approximately two-thirds of the seats in the House of Commons since 1997, has resulted in increasing calls for reform of the House of Commons as well as the House of Lords.

The House of Commons consists of the Members of Parliament (MPs) who are elected by us at general elections. They represent us in making the laws by which this country is governed. Members of Parliament create and discuss proposals for laws (bills) before they become legally binding Acts of Parliament. Members of Parliament should also act as a check (or brake) on the Executive (the Prime Minister and the Cabinet) and try to ensure that the Executive is doing its jobs properly and acting in the interests of the people of this country.

Many people would like to change the existing situation because they argue that MPs do not act as a check on the Prime Minister and the Cabinet. The MP's role is limited; they can ask questions but sometimes receive misleading answers. Members of Parliament can join committees and make recommendations, but the Government does not have to follow them.

Role of the House of Commons

- Acting as a check on government.
- To scrutinize what the government does.
- To ask questions of Ministers, including the Prime Minister.
- Participating in law making: putting forward proposals for legislation, proposing amendments to legislation, scrutinizing legislation, voting for or against new legislation.
- Debating new legislation.
- Representing the interests of their constituents.

Question

Do you regard the UK as a pluralistic parliamentary democracy? Give the reasons for your answer.

Theories of power

There are alternative theories of power.

Elite theory

Classical elite theories reject democracy and assume that in any political system a few will lead the majority. In other words, there will always be a small self-conscious elite with power and a large mass that has very little power.

All societies generally have a social structure, where *oligarchy* (the rule of the few) is inescapable. In addition, most classical elite theorists assume that the masses are psychologically inadequate and therefore unable to hold power. In addition, the masses also have an instinctual need to be dominated. Only the elite can satisfy that need. Robert Michels has termed this 'The Iron Law of Oligarchy'. From this perspective, democracy is not a realistic choice for any political system.

Vilfredo Pareto (1847–1939) begins his analysis with a theory of non-logical actions. He argues that all individuals have six basic instincts, which he terms 'residues'. These are:

- residues of combination – all human beings have an instinct to live together in groups;
- persistence of aggregates – once a group is set up, that community will have an instinctual need to preserve it;
- sentiments of activity – individuals strengthen the bonds that hold groups together by performing ceremonies;
- residues of sociality – all people have an instinctual hostility towards outsiders and a need for uniformity;
- self-preservation – all people have an instinct to preserve their own safety, possessions and social standing;
- sexuality – sexuality has a part to play in sustaining the social control within society.

The elite manipulates these residues via the use of four political procedures that Pareto names the derivations:

- simple assertion – the elite directly pronounces that something is correct, and this is accepted as a adequate explanation;
- authority – the masses agrees to what they are told by the elite because they believe that elite power is legitimate;
- sentiments or principles – the mass embraces elite decisions because they believe such decisions are in agreement with widely held public feelings;

- the persuasive reasoning of the elite convinces the mass.

For Pareto, the elite can choose to rule by their cunning or by the use of force; as he suggests, the elite can either conduct themselves as 'foxes' or 'lions'.

Gaetano Mosca (1858–1911) was also anti-democratic and argued that society should be separated into a small well-organized elite with its own collective aspirations and a large mass, which has no structure and no common aims or aspirations. Mosca outlines several types of elite group: military; priestly; wealthy and landowners. In addition, although the elite may have a control of lawful violence, it does not keep their elite position by use of violence alone. The elite strives to maintain its rule by use of political opinions that are regarded by the mass as common sense or just. It is this manipulation of the ideas of the mass that provides the elite with their source of legitimacy.

In Mosca's view, elites are fundamental for the continuance of the civilized world. The elite holds back social forces that can destroy civilization. Within any society there are a number of conflicting and competing social forces and the stability of a community can be measured by the competence of the elite to restrain these social forces. The elite attempt to do this by imposing a 'political formula'. This political formula is a set of doctrines which if established should bring about political stability. In Britain the political formula would include the principle of 'government by due process of law'.

In terms of critique, Pareto does not clearly define his key terms, for example a residue can be a sentiment, an instinct or a principle. The theory of non-logical actions is diminished by this inability to be clear on these terms. In addition, he provides no picture of the structure of institutions, and very few practical political situations are discussed. Mosca is also unclear on many of his key terms, for example the idea of a social force; in addition he too does not give many examples from everyday practical politics. However, what many people find offensive about elite theory is that it has been used as a justification for fascism.

Marxist theories of power

From the Marxian viewpoint, if a group possess the means of production, not only does it have economic power – it also possesses political power. The state's role is to organize capitalist society in the best interests of the capitalists. The legitimacy of the capitalist system is maintained by ideology. In other words, working-class people are said to have ideas and beliefs that are not in their own economic interests. The media, schools and religion, amongst other institutions, ideologically manipulate the working class.

Ralph Miliband argues that there is a well-organized capitalist class, which controls top posts in both industry and government. Most of these people were educated in top private schools before going on to Oxford or Cambridge. This narrow group of individuals uses the state as an instrument for its own lasting capitalist supremacy.

Nicos Poulantzas, in contrast, argues that the class background of people in the highest governmental posts is unimportant. The organization of society is capitalist, and the role of the state is to sustain capitalism. The state must have a significant degree of autonomy, or independence, from separate capitalists so as to be able to effectively select between the rival requirements for state action from various capitalist interests. The state, in other words, is always necessary for satisfying or fulfilling the wants and needs of capital, even though individual members of top public organizations may not be from a highest-class backgrounds.

analyse this

For Marxists, economic factors determine the nature of political activity; this is termed 'economic determinism'. Discuss with other students what you believe is the significance of gender and race in the political system. What other divisions between people do you think are significant within any political system?

Antonio Gramsci abandoned the 'economic determinism' contained in the type of Marxist analysis that Poulantzas is suggesting. Working from his prison cell in the 1930s, Gramsci suggested a division between two parts of the state: *political society*, which included all the oppressive governmental organizations such as the police and the military, and *civil society*, which consisted of all the organizations which were involved in the production and distribution of ideology, in other words, attempting to manipulate people's ideas and beliefs.

The capitalist state rules by consensus. However, it has the capability to use violence if required. Nevertheless, the state would always want to deal with others by using its bargaining skills to bring forward a settlement. The state strives to form a *historic bloc,* which entails striking a balance with distinct groups in an attempt to preserve society wide feelings of togetherness. Agreement is sustained by *hegemony* – Gramsci's reformulation of the Marxian notion of ideology, a core of belief that becomes a key component of our consciousness and that we interpret as legitimate. Challenging and replacing hegemony with a new historic bloc can only remove capitalism.

In contrast, Abercrombie, Turner and Hill reject approaches that stress the ideological appearance of state power. There are many studies, they suggest, which demonstrate that working-class people discard a dominant ideology: Paul Willis's study *Learning to Labour*, for example, clearly demonstrates how a bunch of working-class lads make an effort to introduce masculine shop-floor culture into the school and renounce the pro-school beliefs that the teachers seek to impose on all school children. Abercrombie and his colleagues, argue that a financial consideration such as anxiety about unemployment is a more important factor in sustaining inequalities within capitalism.

analyse this

What is the role of violence in the political system: for Marxists and for elite theorists? What are the similarities and differences between Marxism and elite theory? Many students wrongly assume that they are one and the same. Later compare your responses against the list below.

Similarities between Marxism and elite theory

- Both Marxism and elite theory have a small ruling class that holds power, and a large group of powerless individuals.
- Both Marxism and elite theory are zero-sum conceptions of power; in other words they presume that there is an unchanging quantity of power in society.
- Both Marxism and elite theory presume that the ruling class sustains its power by manipulating the thoughts and ideas of the powerless.

Differences between Marxism and elite theory

- In the Marxian analysis the dominant class is invariably an economic class; in elite theory this is not the case.
- Marxism has a very promising view of the future – the powerless will one day arise from their exploitation and take power. In elite theory, oligarchy (the rule of the few) is inescapable; the mass will never rise up and take power.
- In the Marxian analysis, the connection between the bourgeoisie and the proletariat is always based upon economic exploitation. In contrast, in elite theory, the masses have a psychological compulsion to be dominated.

- Marxism is used as a political defence for socialism. In contrast, elite theory is used as a political apology for fascism.

State-centred theories

In state-centred explanations, the state is understood to be the most powerful organization in society and it is believed to have interests of its own and to behave in such a way as to bring about these interests. The modern state is not therefore the product of capitalism, or of class relations. There is no power in society pushing the state in any specific direction. Michael Mann suggests that there are several sources of social power: the economic, the political, the military and the ideological. Military dangers from the outside world are one of the most important considerations in any theory of state formation. The state is the only organization that can exercise power in a centralized territorial manner. Eric Nordlinger argues that the state can expand the degree of independence from other groups within the nation by:

- the use of concealed methods of decision making;
- manipulation of the honours system, to provide employment or government contracts with private companies to persuade people to accept its policies and programmes;
- making use of the state's assets to overcome opponents, for example the increased use of government advertising in Britain since 1979;
- changing policy.

One of the most persuasive state-centred theorists is Theda Skocpol who describes a number of states behaving independently to fulfil their own interests. As with Gramsci, whom we discussed above, she suggests that whether a state matures into a powerful independent body or not depends upon how well organized other interests are in society. In contrast to the Marxian analysis, states do not have to represent the interests of the bourgeoisie. A powerful state can shape the action of all classes, including the bourgeoisie.

However, state-centred theorists are often vague about their theoretical assumptions upon which their analysis is based. Although they are critical of the assumptions of Marxists, pluralists and elite theorists, they do not make clear their own assumptions about the links between the state and society clear. At times they are neo-Weberian in nature, at times they are neo-Marxist in nature. In addition, as we have seen in the discussion of Weber and the Marxist theorists, Weber discusses state bureaucrats as having an independence from party politics, and a number of Marxists discuss the 'relative autonomy' of the state.

analyse this

In the summer of 2000 the Conservative Party announced a set of proposals for the reform of Parliament. Read the passage below, list the points you agree with from the summary of the Norton Report and list the points you disagree with and then answer the two questions.

Background

This is a Conservative Party commission set up under the chairmanship of Lord North of Louth (Professor Philip Norton – professor of politics at Hull).

Headline

Calling for a 'big bang' reform of Parliament – a series of individual reforms that could be implemented during the next Parliament.

House of Commons

The Chamber

Want the Chamber 'to be restored to its position as the indisputable arena in which government can be challenged and embarrassed'.

Want MPs and Ministers brought back to the Chamber.

Prime Minister's question time to be restored as twice weekly events each of 30 minutes.

Emphasis on depth not breadth in question time.

More short debates, more of the parliamentary timetable in hands of select committees.

Incentives to make parliamentary life more attractive for backbenchers, committees.

Want to see them strengthened as the vital tools of detailed scrutiny.

Appointment of members should be taken out of the hands of whips.

Change in formula for appointing members.

More resources for select committees.

Greater opportunity to bring issues to floor of House.

Greater role for committees in scrutinizing government spending plans.

Public Audit Committee (see below).

Petitions Committee (see below).

Special standing committees for consideration of Bills should be norm not exception (and in Lords too).

The Opposition

Greater but more targeted resources so that specialists and researchers can be appointed.

'Short money' should be reformed to distinguish between opposition parties and back-bench organizations of parliamentary parties.

Parliamentary parties

Back-bench committees should be provided with modest resources to enable them to carry out functions.

Reforms to make back-bench committees more attractive than all-party groups of MPs.

Need for alternative career structure to front-bench service.

Select committee chairmen to have salaries and staff equivalent to Minister of State.

Chairman of public accounts committee should have salary equivalent to Cabinet Minister.

Each committee should have a vice-chairman and the ability to create subcommittees.

Training courses for new MPs in tools of parliamentary scrutiny.

Technology should be 'exploited rigorously to the benefit of MPs'.

House of Lords

Expand existing number of expert committees.

Particular role on constitutional affairs – envisage a committee working through sub-committees, for example on devolution.

Special role to play scrutinizing cross-cutting subjects, such as social policy and macro-economic policy.

Legislative scrutiny

Primary legislation

Publication of draft Bills as the norm, sent to select committees for pre-legislative scrutiny.

After second reading Bills should stand referred – unless the House votes otherwise – to evidence-taking special standing committees.

Some cross-cutting Bills should be considered by joint committee of both Houses.

Carrying over of Bills should be the norm with proviso that Bills must be enacted within fourteen months of date of second reading.

A new legislation programme committee should determine on what days the stages of a Bill should be taken.

Departmental select committees should be encouraged to engage in post-legislative scrutiny.

Delegated legislation

Statutory instruments should be published in draft.

'Sifting' committee to consider the merits of statutory instruments.

Instruments to be considered in committee on substantive motions.

Recommend use of conditional amendments – Parliament could reject statutory instruments while indicating what would be acceptable if the instrument was to be re-laid.

European legislation

Scrutiny reserve should be embodied in statute.

European Standing Committees to be strengthened and close link with floor of the House.

Scheduling of floor debates should rest with legislation programme committee rather than government.

Changes to prevent departments adding to directives thereby making them more stringent or bringing in directives earlier than necessary.

Financial scrutiny

Tax-management measures should be introduced separately from Finance Bill.

Tax-reform committee on which some MPs should sit.

Main estimates submitted to departmental select committees, each committee to make a report to the House and to have power to recommend the transfer of funds from one heading to another.

Audit commission to be brought within remit of Parliament – a new public audit committee should consider its reports.

National statistics office to be established with director who serves as an officer of Parliament.

Constraining government

Government has grown, as have the numbers of ministers and special advisors – this is bad for government and bad for Parliament.

Cabinet should be capped at 20 members.

Reduction of one-quarter in junior ministers.

Cap on number of Parliamentary private secretaries.

Introduction of a structured parliamentary timetable with established pattern of sittings.

Legislative programme committee (as above)

Both House should resolve that 'any announcement of public policy, requiring legislation or substantial expenditure, should be made by minister to Parliament'

Parliamentary Investigations Officer to investigate cases where information is withheld from Parliament.

Civil servants to be given training processes and requirements of Parliament and Civil Service Code to be amended to require officials to supply information to which MPs are entitled promptly.

Allocation of accommodation to be taken away from whips and given to committee of the House.

Constitutional change

Upper House to play major role in considering implications of constitutional legislation and review constitutional change.

Bill certified by the Speaker as a Bill affecting England exclusively (or England and Wales exclusively) should stand referred to a Bill grand committee, to meet in the chamber and comprise all MPs from England (or England and Wales).

Then to a standing committee with MPs drawn, proportionate to party strength, from English (or English and Welsh) constituencies.

Report stage in grand committee (as above).

Bill then for third reading (i.e. to Commons) but 'we expect a convention to develop at this stage, that MPs from those parts of the UK not affected by the bill will not take part in any division.'

Greater access to Parliament

Increase in MPs office cost allowance with part ring-fenced to employ constituency staff.

Look to greater use, for example, of CABx and local government to reduce constituency casework.

Petitions committee to receive petitions and with power to refer them to appropriate select committee or to undertake enquiries of its own.

Greater access to Palace for the media and more facilities available.

Moving ahead

Once these changes have bedded in, favour a reduction in number of MPs to at least 500 on a staggered basis

Consideration should be given to referring bills to committee before they are taken on the floor of the House

(Source: adapted from www.charter88.org.uk/pubs/brief/0007norton.html)

Questions

1. What is the House of Commons for?
2. How do we make sure it does its job properly?

analyse this

Search the internet for web pages about Charter 88. In what ways does the Norton Report differ from the position of Charter 88? A good starting point is www.charter88.org.uk/.

The 'new' politics

The global changes that we described in the chapter on the information society have led many researchers to suggest that politics has changed significantly and that the traditional theories of power are no longer valid.

The 'new' politics involve a number of major shifts in how we view the political relationships in the world:

- a new foundation for authority and a need to re-evaluate the sociological established theories of authority such as Weber;
- a shift away from class-based politics to identity politics;
- a shift of support from old social movements such as political parties to new social movements;
- the declining significance of the nation state in the face of processes of globalization;
- a loss of faith in big ideologies such as socialism.

This situation can bring with it new forms of community, which may well be very rewarding and very fulfilling for the individuals involved. However, this condition can also generate new forms of hostility towards individuals or groups who are seen to be outsiders; and because human behaviour is free from rationality, the scope for misunderstanding human behaviour and intentions is almost infinite.

According to Zygmunt Bauman, politics today has four characteristics:

- tribal politics – individuals come together with others who they feel share a similar identity; often these communities are nationalistic in nature and are referred to as *tribes* or imagined *communities*;

- politics of desire: individuals need to obtain tribal tokens, for example something trivial like wearing the right kind of clothes, or something more unpleasant like involvement in ethnic cleansing, to show that they are part of the community;
- politics of fear – this is concerned with avoidance of potentially harmful effects, new political issues emerge which have nothing to do with social class, for example the possible link between BSE and CJD;
- politics of certainty – we have a need for expert advice, but today we are unwilling to place our trust in experts. Loss of trust becomes a major political issue.

Questions

1. Do we live in a pluralistic parliamentary democracy? Outline the reasons for your answer.
2. Does the nation state have a role to play in the world today, or has it become largely redundant?
3. Should Britain give up more of its national sovereignty to international bodies, such as the European Union?

8

Political parties

Since the end of the Second World War in 1945, the Labour Party and the Conservative Party have dominated politics in Britain. What do these parties stand for and what are their philosophies or ideologies?

New Labour – what does it stand for?

For many people, Tony Blair is more right wing than most Conservative Prime Ministers in the twentieth century. For others, Blair stands for sound bites, shallowness and broken promises. The term 'social exclusion' has come to be clearly associated with the 'Blair project'. However, the question remains: what does Tony Blair stand for? What is behind the sound bites? What is the Blair Project? The remoralization of Britain? The rebuilding of communities?

Blair has introduced a communitarian strand into British politics and has changed our conception of citizenship significantly.

When Tony Blair became leader of the Labour Party he realized that the public may be unwilling to pay for the level of welfare provision that it had come to expect during the latter half of the twentieth century. Blair also assumed that individual people are 'human agents'. In other words, individual people are responsible for their own actions; individual people make their own choices and determine the course of their own lives. People can choose to do good or they can choose evil.

In particular, he perceived young people as lacking in morality, ambition, and employable skills; in addition, young people had poor manners, were not courteous, did not meet deadlines, were lazy, and were in need of remoralization.

key terms

communitarianism

Communitarianism as an ideology is neither left wing nor right wing. A combination of free-market individualism from the Thatcher–Reagan years and the state planning of the 1945–51 Labour governments, communitarianism is concerned with the responsibility of the individual to the community.

In the early 1990s an image of young people emerged in popular film and television that Henry Giroux has referred to as 'border youth'. The characteristics of border youth were that they had few secure psychological, economic or intellectual markers. As Giroux explains, such youths were condemned: 'to wander across, within, and between multiple borders and spaces marked by excess, otherness, difference, and a dislocating notion of meaning and attention'. Young people, argues Giroux, randomly move from one place to the next with no sense of where they have come from or where they are going. Alienation is driven inward and emerges in comments like, 'I feel stuck'. Irony slightly overshadows a refusal to imagine any kind of collective struggle. Reality seems too desperate to care about. In Giroux's opinion, this vision of youth was seen in such films as *River's Edge* (1986), *My Own Private Idaho* (1991) and *Slackers* (1991). We could add to this list films such as *Bill and Ted's Excellent Adventure* (1992) and the popular television programme and film *Wayne's World.*

In contrast to current belief and practice of all other post-war governments, the Blair government believes that the community should become a 'stakeholder' in all its children. At the moment, the decision to have a child is a personal act, which is of no concern to anyone other than the prospective parents. In addition, in recent years divorce laws have become more 'open', making divorce much easier to obtain. Moreover, during the 1990s parents have had to spend much more time at work. As a consequence, many parents are said to be neglecting their duties as parents; this argument has been most fully developed in one of the major influences upon Blair's thinking, American sociologist Amitai Etzioni's book *The Parenting Deficit.*

According to Etzioni, communitarianism is:

> *dedicated to the betterment of our moral, social, and political environment . . . and [is] dedicated to working with . . . fellow citizens to bring about the changes in values, habits, and public policies that will allow us to do for society what the environmental movement seeks to do for nature: to safeguard and enhance our future.*

The notion of communitarianism can be seen as an attempt to rebuild the idea of 'the community' within an uncertain world where cultures and morality appear to be fragmented and individuals can select any identities they wish – lesbian, gay, green, vegan and so forth. Most importantly, belonging to a neighbourhood with a sense of 'community' appears to have become a thing of the past. In Blair's view our most cherished institutions, such as marriage, the family, and even friendship, have become fragile.

Although Blair has yet to use the term in his fight with lone parents, the disabled and others in receipt of benefit, like all communitarians Blair accepts the principle of *subsidiarity* in which the responsibility for any problem should first be the concern of the individuals nearest the problem. In the case of the lone parent, financial help should be given by the father; if not the father then the immediate family; if not the immediate family then the extended family of aunts, uncles, grandparents and so forth. If the resolution of any problems cannot be achieved, then and only then should the responsibility for solving problems fall onto the community with the state becoming involved.

In a similar fashion, when Blair said that his priority for the Labour Government was 'education, education and education', what he had in mind was the notion of the community as a 'stakeholder' in the community's children. While at school, children should learn how to become 'active' citizens. Children should learn, at the community's expense, how to manage relationships, what it means to be in love, parenting skills, money management and a host of other life skills that any community should reasonably expect its citizens to have.

In contrast to the American influences, the late Scottish philosopher John Macmurray (whom Blair met during his time at Oxford University) and sociologist Anthony Giddens (the current director of the London School of Economics) have influenced Blair's central political and moral views.

John Macmurray

A community is a group of persons, and each person is capable of making a difference in the world. For Macmurray, when we act we bring about a change in the world and all action involves choice. Before we make our choice we have to consider the possible consequences of our actions, which will be either 'good' or 'bad'. To behave in a moral fashion is doing the good knowing that we have the freedom to act otherwise.

The individuals who form a community are united in a common life, they act together and they create an association or a fellowship. In other words, there is more to a community than simply a common purpose, it assumes love and a consciousness of the common life. This consciousness is to be found within all personal associations in a community. An individual carries out actions that can either help or hinder others, as Macmurray explained, 'the morality of an action is inherent in action itself.' Within the community the freedom of each person is dependent upon the intentions of each other individual within the community, as my freedom is dependent upon you acting in a way that does not constrain or harm me. This interdependence of persons, for Macmurray, is the foundation for morality.

From this Macmurray suggests that there are three forms of morality:

- The *communal mode*. This rests upon a positive motivation, to act in a way that benefits others without benefiting oneself. This communal way of behaving reinforces the bonds of community. Therefore, to act in a communal way is regarded as a 'positive' form of morality because it involves actively bringing about a change for the better.

- The *contemplative mode*. This is concerned with 'fitting in' to the ways of behaving that are regarded as normal or acceptable within the community. In many respects this would appear to have more in common with manners than morality. This contemplative mode is regarded as a 'negative' mode of morality, because it involves not acting in a way that may be seen as to the disadvantage of the community.
- The *pragmatic mode* of morality takes the form of obedience or a morality of self-control. Individuals limit their own independence for the benefit the community.

Anthony Giddens

Anthony Giddens is currently director of the London School of Economics and is widely believed to be a significant influence upon New Labour thinking. In a similar fashion to Macmurrray, Giddens also gives a central role to the human agent in his theorizing. Giddens combines theories of social action with theories of social structure in a process known as 'structuration'. The notion of structuration is the idea that individual people create structures in society by creating rules and routines to give our lives meaning.

For Giddens, in the twentieth century we witnessed a move from emancipatory politics to life politics.

Emancipatory politics has two main elements:

- an effort to break free from the restraints of the past;
- overcoming illegitimate domination (coercion), which unfavourably affects the life chances of individuals.

Life politics comes out of emancipatory politics and is a politics of self-actualization. In other words, life politics is about the unhindered creation of a self that you are happy with. If you wish to be gay, straight, a new-age traveller or an office worker, you should be free to do so without others making judgements about you.

The 'third way'

According to New Labour thinking, the 'third way' is a new and improved attitude towards politics, which is said to be neither right wing nor traditional left wing. Influenced by communitarianism, the 'third way' is about fundamentally changing our thinking about citizenship. Traditionally 'citizenship' was something that people were 'given' as of 'right'. Under New

Labour 'citizenship' has become something that people must 'achieve' through work and other contributions to the community. In addition, the 'third way' is about the creation of a 'social investment state', by doing away with social exclusion and segregation. The social investment state attempts to create this new form of community through training and reskilling the young unemployed by the use of programmes such as the 'New Deal' and 'Conexions Gateway'.

For Giddens, people at the bottom of the class ladder have become increasingly excluded from social and political life. The children of poor people are much less likely to stay on at school or college after the age of 16 and have fewer opportunities to move up the class ladder and obtain better-paid jobs. In a similar fashion, increasingly people with well-paid professional and managerial jobs exclude themselves from public institutions, they do not make use of the NHS, their children do not make use of state schools.

Social democracy	**Neoliberalism**	**Third way**
(the old left)	(the new right)	(the centre-left)
Class politics of the left	Class politics of the right	Modernising movement of the centre
Old mixed economy	Market fundamentalism	New mixed economy
Corporatism: state dominates over civil society	Minimal state	New domocratic state
Internationalism	Conservative nation	Cosmopolitan nation
Strong welfare state, protecting 'from cradle to grave'	Welfare safety net	Social investment state

Source: Giddens 'After the left's paralysis', *New Statesmen* 1 May 1998, p.18

The 'New Deal'

'New Deal' was one of Labour's election promises. The purpose of 'New Deal' was to cut 'youth unemployment' through a programme of 'welfare to work'. The central idea behind the programme was to help young people aged between 18 and 24 years of age who had been out of work and claiming benefit for over six months to get jobs. After an initial interview, the young unemployed will be invited into the 'Gateway', a four-month period of personal assessment, in which they have to look at possible reasons why they cannot find work and to identify what they are capable of doing. It is at this stage that any difficulties such as literacy can

be dealt with and also any personal problems such as drug or alcohol abuse can be identified as well as possible rehabilitation strategies.
After the Gateway there are four options open to the young person:

- work in the private or public sector;
- work in the voluntary sector;
- work with the Environmental Task Force – cleaning rubbish from rivers, cleaning graffiti and so forth;
- full-time education or training.

An unemployed person does not have to choose to go into the Gateway, or choose one of the four options. However, refusal will result in a loss of benefits.

analyse this

Clause Four

In 1996 the Labour Party decided to change Clause Four of its constitution. Look at the old and the new Clause Four. What do you believe the old Clause Four stood for? What do you believe the new Clause Four stands for?

The old Clause Four stated:

To secure for the workers by hand or by brain the full fruits of their industry and the most equitable distribution thereof that may be possible upon the basis of the common ownership of the means of production, distribution and exchange, and the best obtainable system of popular administration and control of each industry or service.

Clause Four of the Labour Party Constitution now states that:

by the strength of our common endeavour we achieve more than we achieve alone, so as to create for each of us the means to realise our true potential and for all of us a community in which power, wealth and opportunity are in the hands of the many, not the few, where the rights we enjoy reflect the duties we owe, and where we live together, freely, in a spirit of solidarity, tolerance and respect.

Is this form of politics too authoritarian? Is the government interfering in the personal lives of individuals in a way that it has never done before?

The Blair government used communitarian ideas to significantly change our conception of citizenship. Before Blair became Prime Minister, citizenship was something that was given to all people who were born in Britain, or who could otherwise make a legitimate claim for a British passport. As a British citizen an individual could draw on the resources of the welfare state, the social security system the education service, local authority housing and so forth. Blair has taken the *given* element out of British citizenship; now citizens have to earn through making a contribution to the community. As the new Clause Four makes clear, if people do not make a contribution to the community then they cannot expect the community to provide them with resources. Blair believes that paid work is morally superior to all the alternatives. Individuals are free to choose any lifestyle that they wish and people should respect others for what they choose to be. However, people who choose a lifestyle that does not have paid work as a central element run the risk of having citizenship rights taken away. Blair makes clear that certain lifestyle choices, notably lone parenting without paid work, will not be funded by the community because they are not acceptable lifestyles. Blair has criminalized the lifestyles of poorer people – people who choose not to work and to live on benefits have been made to feel morally inferior to the rest of the community and for them citizenship is denied.

The Conservative Party

Thatcherism

Margaret Thatcher has dominated Conservative philosophy or ideology since the 1970s. With the election of the first Thatcher government in 1979, the New Right philosophy of minimal state involvement and private market solutions to solving social problems became politically acceptable. It is commonly assumed that Mrs Thatcher broke the post-war consensus established by the Labour government of Attlee (1945–51). The 'post-war' consensus was based upon the redistribution of income via the tax and benefits systems, and the establishment of healthcare and education free at the point of issue as central elements in a comprehensive welfare state.

When Margaret Thatcher became Prime Minister in 1979 she described herself not as the first woman to hold the office but as the first scientist. On the doorstep of 10 Downing Street she made her first statement as Prime Minister, a quote from St Francis of Assisi: 'Where there is discord may we bring harmony, where there is error may we bring truth, where there is doubt may we bring faith, and where there is despair may we bring hope.'

This was the first of many interesting and thought-provoking sound bites from a politician who was to give her name to a political doctrine – 'Thatcherism' – and who was to break the mould of British politics. Anybody who lived through the Thatcher years will have their favourite quotations from Mrs Thatcher. Mine include: 'No one would remember the Good Samaritan if he'd only had good intentions. He had money as well.'

Under the leadership of Mrs Thatcher from 1975 to 1990, the Conservatives became closely associated with 'New Right' ideas. These included:

- an emphasis on personal liberty and personal freedom;
- the free market and opposition to state planning;
- popular capitalism – notably privatization and home ownership;
- the promotion of the normal heterosexual family;
- reduction of public spending;
- giving people incentives to work by lowering both taxes and benefits;
- making people less dependent upon the welfare state.

For New Right thinkers the welfare state removed freedom and responsibility, reduced incentives, produced waste, promoted social grievances and removed individual freedom. In other words, the welfare state produced a dangerous underclass.

Conservative Party leaders that followed Thatcher, notably John Major, did not abandon the Thatcherite politics totally but moved towards improving standards of service provision in the public sector, with the citizens' charter.

At the level of rhetoric, Thatcherism was seen as conviction politics, as enterprise culture pushing back the 'nanny state', as giving unions back to their members. Many on the left, notably sociologists such as Stuart Hall, came to view Thatcherism as 'authoritarian populism' where Thatcher recreated common sense in the minds of the working class by the use of 'hegemonic messages'.

Dennis Kavanagh, in his book *Thatcherism and British Politics: The End of Consensus?*, provides perhaps the clearest statement on Thatcherism as a major break with the post-war consensus. For Kavanagh, Thatcherism contained both style and policy. At the level of style, Thatcherism was based upon the distinct personality of Mrs Thatcher herself. At the level of policy, Thatcherism stressed control of the money supply to control inflation; the reduction of the public sector (or 'privatization'); freeing the labour market through reform and the restoration of the government's authority.

In a similar fashion, Philip Norton (1987) suggested three propositions about Mrs Thatcher:

- she changed the nature of the political debate in Britain;

- she imposed her will upon government policy and dominated Cabinet;
- institutions that were seen as obstacles were abolished or reformed.

S.E. Finer (1987) explained that all post-war governments accepted the triangle of public corporations, social services and full employment. However, the Thatcher government had a very different vision of politics and the role of government:

- Keynesian deficit financing was out;
- physical controls and/or subsidies to ailing industries were out;
- in came money-supply economics and financial management of the economy;
- unions were cold-shouldered;
- public expenditure was restrained;
- nationalized industries were told to make profits;
- privatization;
- exchange controls were abolished;
- the maximum possible scope was given to market forces.

Finer explains: 'nothing – neither the rising unemployment that had stricken Macmillan and Heath with panic, or waves of strikes such as had paralysed former governments – simply nothing was allowed to stand in the way of these policies.'

In many respects this was because, from a Thatcherite perspective, unemployment was blamed upon the unemployed themselves. They had priced themselves out of jobs by demanding higher wages.

In a similar fashion to Kavanagh and Finer, other writers argued that Thatcher brought about a major change in values, attitudes and beliefs. Stephen Haseler, for example, in his 1989 book *The Battle for Britain: Thatcher and the New Liberals,* argued that Thatcherism was a reaction to the dominant paternalist stance of the major political parties in Britain from 1945 onwards. We could add that Mrs Thatcher attempted to turn the political into the personal. 'Don't spend more than you earn' became economic policy; 'Don't trust foreigners' became foreign policy. Is this the hallmark of a postmodern politics?

The New Right under Thatcher was in favour of a return to 'Victorian values' – a throwback to the Margaret Thatcher's schooldays under the paternalistic eye of Alderman Roberts. A return to 'Victorian values' came to mean privatization of the welfare state. Instead of having 'collective' or state provision there was more private insurance, for health and pensions; more contracting out of school and hospital cleaning and hospital services; the introduction of a voucher system for nursery education and the replacing of student grants by student loans. The idea behind these moves was to make people less dependent upon the state and more independent. Like pluralists, the New Right believes that the state should be both 'rule maker' and 'umpire'. In other words the state should police things like the market, looking for market imperfections such as large companies fixing prices, and so forth.

According to Julian Le Grand (1986) the welfare state includes:

- a social security system that shifts cash from taxpayers to people on benefit;
- a number of 'benefits in kind'– these are provided 'free' by the state because they are considered 'good' for society and include: health-care, education and a range of 'personal social services' such as the services of social workers, home helps and 'meals on wheels';
- there is also a range of price subsidies designed to reduce the cost to consumers of certain goods that were thought to be 'socially desirable' – these included rent subsidies, housing improvement grants and public transport subsidies.

Before the success of the New Right, the state was involved in social and economic activities in three ways: by direct provision, subsidy and regulation.

Privatization (the reduction in state involvement), in which the New Right clearly believes, was also of three types:

- reduction of state provision – for example the sale of council houses;
- reduction of state subsidy – for example increases in charges for school trips; charges for NHS services; the replacement of student grants with loans and the introduction of tuition fees for university students;
- reduction of state regulation – for example the deregulation of the bus services.

According to New Right thinkers, these changes are in the interests of efficiency.

Vic George and Paul Wilding give a very full and clear outline of the New Right philosophy in 1982. They argue that New Right thinkers such as Hayek, Friedman and Powell believe in what was known, in the nineteenth century, as liberalism. The New Right are opposed to state intervention, which they term 'collectivism', and also believe in freedom or liberty, individualism and inequality.

Freedom or liberty is seen in negative terms. People are free if they are not under coercion. In other words, if people are not forcing you to do something that you do not want to do then you are free.

In addition, these New Right thinkers believe that all people are irrational and unreliable. However, if they make mistakes then it only affects a small group of people. In contrast, if the head of a government, who is also a person and also irrational and unreliable, were to make a big planning decision that went wrong, then millions of people would suffer.

The New Right also believes in inequality. Inequality is good because it provides people with incentives to better themselves. In contrast, the state can only bring about equality by coercion or force – by taking money away from people in the form of taxes which people are unwilling to pay. In addition, state intervention is socially disruptive because, according to Enoch Powell, the welfare state turns 'wants' into 'rights'. I might want healthcare, I might want my children to be educated, and I might want social security. However, if the state cannot afford to provide these things then I will feel that my 'rights' have been ignored and I might turn to violence or crime to get what I believe is mine as of right.

Moreover, from a New Right perspective, state services are wasteful of resources. State services are usually provided free of charge to the person using them so people consume as much as they possibly can. As state services have to be paid for out of taxes then there is always a lack of concern over individual freedom.

Under the leadership of John Major, William Hague and Iain Duncan Smith, the Thatcherite project was not abandoned. However, the Conservative leaders that followed Thatcher gave much greater emphasis to finding value for money in the public services by imposing bureaucratic quality assurance systems. John Major introduced the notion of Charter Rights (such as the Further Education Charter, which explains all the rights that students can expect from their FE College) in all areas of public service.

There are, however, question marks about the monetarist credentials of the Thatcher governments. Sir Geoffrey Howe and Nigel Lawson did have great difficulty controlling the money supply. Lawson changed the treasury definition of money from the broad M3 definition to the much narrower M0 definition. In addition, the Treasury Select Committee challenged Nigel Lawson in 1985 on the grounds that government had undergone a U-turn in monetarist policy – that the Chancellor had abandoned control of the money supply in managing the economy, instead placing a greater emphasis on the use of interest rates and greater government spending to stimulate demand. As Paul Hirst argued:

> *Mrs Thatcher threw away monetarism, the apparent core of her ideas in 1979, when it became a political liability. She did the biggest 'U' turn of any modern conservative politician: proving herself to be at once more pragmatic than Stanley Baldwin and more cynical than Harold Macmillan – both hard acts to follow.*

In other words, Mrs Thatcher was logically motivated rather than motivated by dogma during her time as Prime Minister.

Politically at least, William Hague has not had a happy time during his period as Conservative Party leader. Why did the Conservative Party fail to make any headway against Labour whilst Hague was Conservative leader?

Hague's top priority was the reform and renewal of his party. One of the possible, and most overlooked, reasons for the success of Tony Blair in May 1997 was the fact that since the 1970s the Conservative Party, as a political organization, has been unable to successfully combat effective opposition. This fact was masked for most of the period by the strong leadership of Mrs Thatcher together with weak and divided opposition: the Labour Party under Michael Foot and the Alliance under David Steel and David Owen.

Conservative Party structure

The functions of the party's national union are:

- to promote the aims of the party;
- to form and develop a Conservative Association in every constituency;
- to act as a link between leader and the party in the country;
- to liaise with Central Office;
- to liaise with the party in Scotland and Wales.

The work of the national union is carried out through a central council, which is the governing body and rule maker of the national union. In addition, an executive committee, a general purposes committee and provincial area councils all have roles to play within the national union. The Conservative Party conference each year is the conference of the national union. It is not clear if the decisions of the conference of the national union are binding on the party and its leadership or if the conference decisions are party policy.

Reform of the Conservative Party

William Hague made the then Asda chief and the Conservative MP Archie Norman a vice-chairman of the party with the job of investigating and advising the Conservative leadership on party structure. In a speech to the Conservative Party Conference, entitled 'Our party: blueprint for change', Archie Norman said that their ambition was not small but to significantly change the structure, all levels, both at Central Office and in the country as a whole. He wanted:

- to double the membership;

- real involvement – 'I want to point to ideas in the next Manifesto that are members' ideas';
- a new Conservative youth movement;
- 25 per cent of women candidates there on merit and selected by the constituency associations;
- to double the number of Conservative councillors; and
- a united party that is open to ideas and debate but intolerant of dishonesty in any form!

Norman asserted that the reform of the Conservative Party should be part of a forward movement in British politics – the creation of a new kind of political party that operates within the community and that urges active commitment from all members, whether they are MPs or local activists, and takes notice of all individual and group contributions to party policy. He summed this up with the phrase: 'Members matter'.

Questions

1. The passage above suggests that one reason why William Hague failed to become Prime Minister during his period of Conservative leadership was because of the weak and ineffective structure of the Conservative Party. Do you accept or reject the reasons outlined in the passage. State the reasons for your answer.
2. In your opinion are the problems that Iain Duncan Smith faces in leading the Conservative Party similar to the problems that William Hague faced? State the reasons for your answer.
3. What do you believe New Labour stands for?
4. When Blair said (in 1996) that his priority for the Labour Government was 'education, education and education' what do you think he meant?
5. Do you accept or reject the principle of *subsidiarity* in which the responsibility for any problem should first be the concern of the individuals nearest the problem? State the reasons for your answer.
6. What are the differences between New Labour's philosophy and Thatcherism?
7. What are the differences between the old Clause Four of the Labour Party constitution and the new Clause Four?
8. What do you understand by the term 'New Deal'? Are you in favour of 'welfare to work' schemes? State the reasons for your answer.

9

Crime

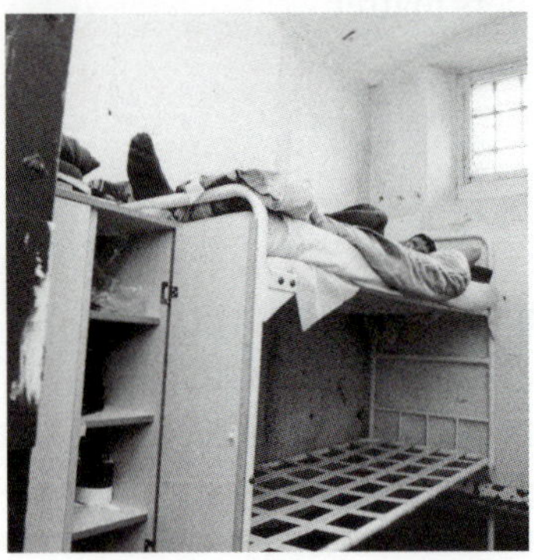

Do people choose to become criminals of their own free will? Or do people become criminals because there are forces outside of their control such as biological factors, psychological factors, race, gender or social class that compel individuals to behave this way? Alternatively, does the criminal justice system apply laws against some groups and downplay infringements by others?

Criminologists make a distinction between 'crimes' and 'deviance'. A crime is committed when a person breaks the law. However, 'deviance' is any act that is disapproved of in a community, irrespective of whether it is criminal or not. Both crime and deviance involve people breaking the accepted standards of behaviour. However, standards of behaviour change over time and from place to place. In other words, deviance is 'relative' in nature. To be naked in the street is both illegal and deviant, but to be naked in the bath is perfectly normal. Streeter, in an article in the *Independent* (29 November 1997), gives a number of examples of laws that are still on the statute book and as such are still technically crimes, but the police do not enforce them. Look at the forms of behaviour below and say which are 'crimes' and which are not:

- to make mince pies on Christmas day;
- to eat mince pies on Christmas day;
- to shout 'taxi' in the street;
- to sell a product or service to a woman on a Sunday.

The answer is that they are all currently crimes, but of course, the police do not enforce such laws and people do not regard such behaviour as either criminal or deviant. How can behaviour that was once illegal now be tolerated? The answer is that what we understand as criminal or deviant behaviour is *culturally determined* – our ideas of what is

key terms

crime

Any behaviour that involves breaking the law.

delinquency

Criminal behaviour carried out by young people.

deviance

Behaving in a way that other people will disapprove of.

acceptable behaviour change over time in a similar way to the changing fashion in relation to clothes and shoes. However, many acts are regarded as criminal and many people feel that they suffer because they are victims of crime.

analyse this

Look at the table below, which outlines the figures for a number of serious notifiable offences (serious offences) from 1991 to 2002.

Recorded crime by offence 1991, 1995 to 2001/02 and percentage change between 2000/01 and 2001/02

Numbers and percentage changes — Recorded crime

	Offence	1991	1995	1996	1997	1997/1998[1]	1998/1999[1]	1998/1999[2]	1999/2000	2000/2001	2001/2002	% change between 2000/2001 and 2001/2002
1 4.1 4.2	Murder Manslaughter Homicide Infanticide	725	745	679	739	748	750	750	766	850	886	4
2	Attempted murder	555	634	674	652	661	676	676	750	708	858	21
3	Threat or conspiracy to murder	4,712	7,044	8,533	9,340	9,661	11,112	11,212	13,434	14,064	13,648	-3
4.3	Child destruction	2	8	2	5	6	9	9	1	2	–	–
4.4 4.6	Causing death by dangerous driving Causing death by careless driving when under the influence of drink or drugs	416	242	320	291	325	348	349	317	335	371	11
37.1	Causing death by aggravated vehicle taking	–	21	34	12	18	30	30	37	35	36	3
5	Wounding or other act endangering life	9,408	10,445	12,169	12,531	12,833	13,960	14,006	15,135	15,662	16,537	6

6	Endangering railway passenger	11	12	12	11	7	15	15	7	10	14	40
7	More serious offences	15,829	19,151	22,423	23,581	24,259	26,900	27,047	30,447	31,666	32,350	2
	Endangering life at sea	–	–	–	–	–	–	–	1	–	4	–
8A	Other wounding							196,737	201,290	195,925	208,586	6
8B	Possession of weapons[3]	174,245	193,016	216,467	226,795	231,360	203,313	23,635	23,792	24,552	28,740	17
8C	Harassment[4]							79,534	88,625	93,832	96,691	3
8D	Racially-aggravated other wounding[5]								2,687	3,176	3,473	9
8E	Racially-aggravated harassment[5]								10,758	12,468	14,986	20
11	Cruelty to or neglect of children[4]	–	–	–	–	–	–	2,300	2,631	2,558	3,048	19
12	Abandoning a child under the age of two years	47	46	65	56	54	41	42	51	48	49	2
13	Child abduction	196	355	374	390	391	490	502	577	546	583	7
14	Procuring illegal abortion	3	5	7	-	-	2	2	2	4	6	50
15	Concealment of birth	19	15	4	5	6	10	10	4	9	3	-67
104	Assault on a constable[4]	–	–	–	–	–	–	21,510	26,115	28,000	30,010	7
105A	Common assault[4]	–	–	–	–	–	–	151,469	189,783	203,427	226,451	11
105B	Racially-aggravated common assault[5]	–	–	–	–	–	–	–	4,275	4,711	5,174	10
	Less serious offences	174,510	193,437	216,917	227,246	231,811	203,856	475,741	550,591	569,256	617,804	9
	Total violence against the person	**190,339**	**212,588**	**239,340**	**250,827**	**256,070**	**230,756**	**502,788**	**581,038**	**600,922**	**650,154**	**8**
16	Buggery	1,127	818	728	645	657	567	566	437	401	354	–12
17	Indecent assault on a male	3,070	3,150	3,130	3,503	3,885	3,672	3,683	3,614	3,530	3,613	2
18	Gross indecency between males	965	727	553	520	483	353	354	286	167	163	–2

19A	Rape of a female	4,045	4,986	5,759	6,281	6,523	7,139	7,132	7,809	7,929	9,008	14
19B	Rape of a male	–	150	231	347	375	502	504	600	664	735	11
20	Indecent assault on a female	15,792	16,876	17,643	18,674	18,979	19,463	19,524	20,664	20,301	21,765	7
21	Unlawful sexual intercourse with a girl under 13	315	178	171	148	156	153	153	181	155	170	10
22	Unlawful sexual intercourse with a girl under 16	1,949	1,260	1,261	1,112	1,084	1,133	1,135	1,270	1,237	1,336	8
23	Incest	389	185	157	183	189	139	139	121	80	93	16
24	Procuration	138	207	132	131	142	155	215	138	129	130	1
25	Abduction	411	364	313	277	258	242	240	251	262	263	–
26	Bigamy	75	86	98	75	106	126	129	83	80	74	–8
27	Soliciting or importuning by a man[4]	–	–	–	–	–	–	1,107	973	1,028	1,648	60
73	Abuse of position of trust[6]	–	–	–	–	–	–	–	–	12	408	–
74	Gross indecency with a child	1,147	1,287	1,215	1,269	1,314	1,271	1,293	1,365	1,336	1,665	25
	Total sexual offences	**29,423**	**30,274**	**31,391**	**33,165**	**34,151**	**34,915**	**36,174**	**37,792**	**37,311**	**41,425**	**11**
34A	Robbery of business property	45,323	68,074	74,035	63,072	62,652	66,172	10,481	12,148	12,394	13,197	6
34B	Robbery of personal property							56,354	72,129	82,760	108,178	31
	Total robbery	**45,323**	**68,074**	**74,035**	**63,072**	**62,652**	**66,172**	**66,835**	**84,277**	**95,154**	**121,375**	**28**
	Total violent crime	**265,085**	**310,936**	**344,766**	**347,064**	**352,873**	**331,843**	**605,797**	**703,107**	**733,387**	**812,954**	**11**

1. The number of crimes recorded in that financial year using the coverage and rules in use until 31 March 1998.
2. The number of crimes recorded in that financial year using the expanded offence coverage and revised counting rules which came into effect on 1 April 1998.
3. Included within 'other wounding' prior to 1 April 1998.
4. These offences were added to the series from 1 April 1998.
5. These offences were added to the series from 1 April 1999, prior to that they would have been included in the original classifications.
6. These offences were added to the series from 1 January 2001.

Source: www.police999.com

Questions

1 Identify what you consider to be the four most serious types of crime and outline the changes that have taken place in the figures over the past 10 years.

2 In general, how would you describe the changing crime figures over the period?

Why do people commit crime?

So why do some people commit crime, when they know that such activities are disapproved of and that the people found guilty will be punished? There are a number of possible explanations.

Biological theories

These explanations argue that some people are genetically more likely to commit crime. Cesare Lombroso (1836–1909) argued that it was possible to identify physical characteristics that were signs of such a genetic predisposition to crime. These included indifference to pain, large ears, extra toes or fingers, a large jaw and high cheekbones. Similarly, Giambattista della Porta (1536–1615) had done similar work on natural magic and demonology as possible causes of crime. Up until the 1950s researchers were attempting to identify the characteristics of the *mesomorph,* the person who was physiologically more inclined to criminal behaviour. However, female criminals were much less likely to show such physical characteristics, except for prostitutes who were found to be much more likely to have thicker thighs. Rather, female criminals were much more likely to be morally deficient.

Psychological theories

These explanations argue that criminal behaviour is a form of sickness rooted in a person's mental processes. Hans Eysenck has argued that there are clear links between genetically determined personality traits and criminal behaviour.

Robert Hare, in his book *The Hare Psychopathy Checklist –Revised*, looked at the available psychological research and identified the following characteristics of the psychopathic personality and behaviour.

- glibness/superficial charm;
- grandiose sense of self-worth;
- need for stimulation/prone to boredom;
- pathological lying;
- cunning/manipulative;
- lack of remorse or guilt;
- shallow emotional response;
- callous/lack of empathy;
- parasitic lifestyle;
- poor behavioural controls;
- promiscuous sexual behaviour;
- early behavioural problems;
- lack of realistic long-term goals;
- impulsivity;
- irresponsibility;
- failure to accept responsibility for their own actions;
- many short-term relationships;
- juvenile delinquency.

The argument here is that it is genetic factors that produces the psychopathic personality either because the brain of a psychopath may function and process information differently from the rest of the population or that psychopathic behaviour arises from a strong genetic predisposition towards self-defence – a form of 'survival of the fittest' instinct.

However, some researchers have pointed to premenstrual tension (PMS) and other hormone imbalances as a possible cause of violence amongst women. Research in the United States by Catrin Smith found that:

> *Accounts from prison healthcare staff indicate that menstrual disorders take up a high proportion of doctors' time in women's prisons, ranking among the conditions most frequently presented for consultation.*
>
> (Source: www.asc41.com/www/2002/absri348.htm)

Criticisms of both the biological and psychological theories would be that:

- they neglect social and cultural factors – for example, crime is associated with a person's class position;
- the term 'psychopath' does not appear in the *Diagnostic and Statistical Manual* of mental disorders (DSM-3), which is published by the American Psychiatric Association and is the main diagnostic reference for mental-health professionals in the US and Europe;
- it is not possible to identify the criminal gene;
- there is no explanation of why 'normal' people commit crime.

There are few reliable measures of poor mental health and the link with criminal behaviour is difficult to prove. Researchers who claim that crime has a psychological basis are using similar arguments to people who claim that deviance is caused by the possession of a person by demons.

analyse this

the trial of Peter Sutcliffe, 'The Yorkshire Ripper'

In 1981 Peter Sutcliffe was convicted of the murder of 13 women. At the start of his trial he attempted to claim that he was suffering from paranoiac schizophrenia and that he would therefore plead guilty not to murder but to manslaughter on the grounds of diminished responsibility. Read the two passages below from the trial. Under what circumstances would *you* accept mental illness as a legitimate motivation for committing a crime? In the case below, the burden of proof is on the accused to prove that he has a mental illness. Is this right and legitimate? Or should the burden of proof be on the prosecution to prove that the accused is sane? Give at least three reasons for your answer. You may find it helpful to read the full transcript at www.execulink.com/~kbrannen/trialall.pdf.

> *When asked his plea on each of the thirteen murder charges, Peter William Sutcliffe pleaded: Not guilty to murder but guilty to manslaughter on the grounds of diminished responsibility.' He also pleaded guilty to each of the seven charges of attempted murder.*

Sir Michael Havers told Mr Justice Boreham that the Crown accepts the pleas by Mr Sutcliffe. He also stated that he has the reports of four psychiatrists who had interviewed Mr Sutcliffe. Sir Michael: 'I have met with them to discuss their reports with the greatest care and anxiety and at great length. The general consensus of the doctors is that this is a case of diminished responsibility, the illness being paranoiac schizophrenia.'

Mr Justice Boreham: 'I have very grave anxieties about Sutcliffe and his pleas. I would like you to explain in far greater detail than usual any decision that you are going to make about the acceptance of these pleas.'

For the next two hours, Sir Michael Havers outlined the reasons why the Crown was prepared to accept the pleas of diminished responsibility, including details of Mr Sutcliffe's history, confessions, conversations with the psychiatrists, the reports by the psychiatrists, and other evidence.

After Sir Michael Havers finished putting his case: 'that this is a case of diminished responsibility', Mr Justice Boreham rendered his decision: 'The matter that troubles me is not the medical opinions because there is a consensus. It seems to me that all of these opinions – and I say this without criticism – all these opinions are based simply on what this defendant has told the doctors, nothing more. Moreover what he has told the doctors conflicts substantially with what he told the police on the morning of arrest. I use the word "conflict" advisedly. In statements to the police he expressed a desire to kill all women. If that is right – and here I really need your help – is that not a matter which ought to be tested? Where lies the evidence which gives these doctors the factual basis for these pleas? It is a matter for the defendant to establish. It is a matter for a jury. We have in a sense conducted a trial which has satisfied us. It seems to me it would be more appropriate if this case were dealt with by a jury.'

Mr Justice Boreham asked Mr Sutcliffe why he had tried to cut off Jean Jordan's head with a hacksaw. Mr Sutcliffe replied: 'Because she was in league with the Devil and between them they had hidden the £5 note and I was going to do the same thing with her head.' Pointing out that Mr Sutcliffe had not found the £5 note, Mr Justice Boreham said: 'I don't want to get into a theological argument, but are you saying that she and her colleague the Devil had beaten you and your God?'

Mr Sutcliffe: 'Yes. It seemed very much so.'

Sir Michael: 'Had you realised by about mid-February that you were not getting on too well in persuading these learned gentlemen that you were fit for the loony bin?'

Mr Sutcliffe: 'No.'

Sir Michael: 'And then did you say: "Right. We'd better pull some more aces out of the pack." The mission was the floater and the bait on the hook was God's message, and they (the doctors) fell for it hook, line and sinker. Is that what happened?'

Mr Sutcliffe: 'No.'

Peter Sutcliffe was briefly re-examined by his defence counsel, James Chadwin, QC, where he again denied that he was trying to feign insanity. He also stated that he had never been told by a doctor that he would only get 10 years if in an asylum.

key terms

In order to fully understand the functionalist and Marxist approaches to crime you need to grasp the following terms:

social order

The structure of society that provides a framework that allows us to experience social life as something that has a predictable feel to it.

social control

A set of ideas and ways of behaving that are imposed upon us and reinforced by sanctions, ranging from disapproval to imprisonment.

Functionalist theories

Functionalist theorists assume that as individuals we live and work within a social system that is made up of individuals who perform roles within institutions and that the social system people share a set of common values. Crime and deviance are seen as examples of the common value system being broken. Often people who have not been socialized effectively by their parents into accepting the common values cause this deviance. Crime and deviance are seen as potentially harmful to the effective functioning of the social system, in other words crime and deviance are potentially dysfunctional. However, such acts can also have a positive benefit for society: they are a demonstration of unhappiness and as such a good warning sign that change is needed. However, people who are unhappy because they feel deprived or frustrated because they lack opportunities to enjoy the style of life that the rest of us take for granted can also cause such acts. Such people may turn to crime for financial benefit, or turn to delinquent subcultures, which offer an illegitimate ladder of success.

Marxist theories

For the Marxist, crime is a reflection of the unjust nature of capitalist society. The purpose of the law, police, the courts is to defend the interests of capitalists. This is reflected in the class composition of the judiciary, the magistrates' bench, barristers and solicitors, the vast majority of whom are drawn from professional upper middle-class families. The law is built upon a dominant ideology that manipulates people's ideas so that they are willing to live in unequal class-based societies. The law serves the interests of the ruling class. In addition, the state (the government and all its supporting agencies) is an agent of social control. Its sole purpose is to maintain the smooth running of capitalist society.

However, critics could point out that:

- the police force is drawn largely from people who come from a working-class background;
- crimes against the person do not have an obvious relationship to capitalism;
- health and safety legislation, employment protection legislation, national minimum wage legislation and equal opportunities legislation can all be see as legislation that benefits working-class people at the expense of capitalists;
- Marxism places a great deal of emphasis upon class division, but ignores other significant divisions in society, such as factors leading to women, young people, ethnic minorities, and lesbians and gays becoming criminals and offenders.

analyse this

If we are to prevent crime in future, we shall have to bring back the element of deterrence. The sociologists have had their day. It is no coincidence that the abolition of capital punishment has resulted in a tenfold increase in crime involving weapons, and a fivefold increase in the number of killings. It is no coincidence that, since the abolition of the cane, our schools have become unruly places with a high degree of truancy, where teachers are frightened to discipline or control the rowdy troublemakers who go on to become the hard-core juvenile offenders. It is also no coincidence that, since cautioning has blossomed and, in some areas, become the standard reaction of the system to wrongdoing, and since guilty pleas to lesser offences have begun to be accepted more and more by the Crown Prosecution Service in the magistrates court, so that cases do not go to the Crown court . . . fewer offenders are frightened about what will happen to them if they are caught.

(Source: Sir Ivan Lawrence, www.parliament.the-stationery-office.co.uk/pa/cm199394/cmhansrd/1993-11-23/Debate-4.html)

Questions

1 Look at each of the perspectives on crime outlined above. For each perspective outline what you believe is the function of punishment.

2 According to the passage above what are the causes of crime? Do you accept or reject the causes suggested? Give four reasons for your answer.

Crime statistics

Since 1857 in England and Wales official records of the number of crimes known to the police have been published. However, on the basis of victim studies and self-report studies such as the British Crime Survey – where people are asked to report the crimes that they have committed and crimes they have been victims of – it is estimated that the real level of crime is much higher than the level of reported crime.

For a detailed look at the British Crime Survey see the following website: www.homeoffice.gov.uk/rds/bcs1.html.

In general, many crimes are not reported to the police because:

- They are thought to be too trivial, 'petty' crimes are much less likely to be reported.
- In April 2001 new rules were introduced for police officers reporting the recording of crime. A reported crime may fall outside of the new rules – for a full outline of the rules look at www.homeoffice.gov.uk/rds/bcs1.html.

Reasons for not reporting crime to the police 2001/02 interviews

Percentages BCS

	Burglary	Thefts from vehicles and attempts	Other household theft	Other personal theft	BCS violence	Comparable subset[2]	All BCS[1]
Trivial/no loss/ police could not do anything[3]	76	82	81	69	46	70	72
Fear of reprisal	6	<1	2	0	7	3	3
Police related reasons[4]	3	2	1	1	2	2	2
Private/dealt with ourselves	21	16	16	14	45	25	22
Reported to other authorities	2	1	1	17	6	3	5
Inconvenient to report	5	7	5	6	4	5	5
Other	2	2	2	3	4	3	3
Unweighted N	382	1378	1165	548	788	4862	6575

1. Source 2001/02 BCS. Don't knows excluded from the base. More than one reason could be given.
2. The comparable crime subset includes vandalism, burglary, vehicle theft, bicycle theft, wounding, common assault, robbery, snatch and stealth theft. Thefts of vehicles not shown as very few incidents were not reported.
3. Trivial/no loss and police could not do anything or would not be interested are merged due to the similarity in their definition, for example: A respondent who thinks the incident was too trivial may code the incident as 'too trivial, no loss' or 'the police would not be interested' as these two codes may be understood as meaning the same.
4. Police-related reasons include: dislike or fear of the police and previous bad experience with the police or courts.

Source: www.police999.com © Crown copyright

- Victims may be embarrassed.
- Victims may be unaware that a crime has been committed against them.
- There may be a lack of confidence in the ability of the police to catch the criminal responsible.
- There may be a fear of reprisal.

- People may decide to take the law into their own hands and deal with the criminal themselves.
- Moral panics may affect the crime rate.

What is a moral panic?

A moral panic is an unexpected but considerable increase in public demand for something to be done about a social problem. In some cases the problem may be a new but real problem that people did not know about previously. In other cases the media may invent the problem. However, the media pay a central role in heightening people's concerns about the issue.

analyse this

dangerous dogs – a moral panic

In the late 1980s there were a number of serious dog attacks in which a number of people were badly injured. During the summer months, when there is traditionally little political or industrial news, the newspapers were often full of stories of dog attacks. People had kept such dogs previously, and such dogs had attacked people before, but this was previously not considered to be newsworthy. The Dangerous Dogs Act 1991, which was replaced by the Dangerous Dogs (Amendment) Act 1997, selected the following dogs as *dangerous dogs*:

- pit-bull terrier – including cross-bred pit-bulls;
- Japanese tosa;
- dogo Argentino;
- fila Braziliero.

It is illegal to possess one of these dogs without a certificate of exemption, which will only be granted if the dog is neutered, insured, and has a transponder implanted. These dogs are not allowed to be in any public place without being muzzled and kept firmly on a lead by a person who is not less than 16 years old. A public place even includes inside a locked car that is in a public place.

A dog of any breed will be regarded as dangerously out of control if a person feels that there are reasonable grounds for believing that the dog will injure any person, whether or not it actually does so. If aggressive dogs are, for example, allowed to intimidate walkers on a public footpath, even if the dogs are on private land and behind a fence, the owner can be prosecuted.

Question

Is the issue of dangerous dogs a moral panic?

Women and crime

If you search through the crime statistics, one of the things that you will find is that in recent years there has been a significant increase in the number of women convicted of criminal offences. However, it is still the case than men are convicted for the vast majority of crimes. Why do women have such a low conviction rate? Several possible explanations have been suggested:

- women go through a process of socialisation that strongly disapproves of toughness and stresses femininity;
- women are under stricter control and have lives that are more tightly regulated, hence women have fewer opportunities to commit crime;
- pressure from female peer groups emphasizes passivity and law-abiding behaviour.

However, it may simply be the case that women are much more effective criminals and are less likely to be caught. Many researchers have suggested that the crime statistics underestimate the degree of women's involvement in crime. Domestic roles give people more opportunity to hide crimes – men who fall down stairs may have been pushed! In places of work, opportunities to commit crime may be greater, but so is the chance of getting caught. Women's liberation and the greater involvement of women in the labour market may be factors in the increase of female crime. Traditionally, it was always argued that the criminal justice system was patriarchal in nature in that the police and the courts were more likely to see women as victims rather than criminals.

In contrast, ethnic minorities are much more likely to be convicted of a crime than the rest of the population. Researchers have suggested that men from ethnic minorities are much more likely to be labelled as criminals and are much more likely to be stopped and searched by the police. African-Caribbean men are much more likely to be unemployed or underemployed and face exclusion and disadvantage, both of which are factors strongly associated with crime.

Questions

1. In your opinion what are the causes of rising crime?
2. Do you find any of the criminological explanations convincing?
3. What do you believe is the purpose of punishment?

index

Page numbers in **bold** indicate where the term has been defined in the text